CONTENTS

INTRODUCTION

Above Before the attacks of 9/11, the Twin Towers of the World Trade Center were the tallest buildings in New York City.

*S*eptember 11, 2001, was almost certainly the single most shocking day in the history of the United States. Without question, it was also among the nation's most tragic days. When 19 terrorists hijacked four US passenger planes that morning, they unleashed a wave of death, injury, destruction and fear within the space of only a few hours.

In terms of the number of lives lost (approximately 3,000 in all four crashes, not counting the terrorists), no act of war by a foreign power — not even the attack by Japan on the US naval base at Pearl Harbor, Hawaii, in 1942 — had ever struck such a blow on US territory.

New Yorkers were stunned when the first hijacked plane flew into the North Tower of the World Trade Center (WTC). Within minutes live televised images of the burning skyscraper were breaking into morning news and talk shows. Many believed it must have been an accident. Minutes later, millions watching the aftermath of the first hit, watched in horror as a second plane hit the South Tower. Few now held onto the belief that what was happening was an accident. As a third plane hit the Pentagon — the headquarters of the US armed forces — outside Washington, D. C., and a fourth crashed in a field in Pennsylvania, no one believed this could be anything but an attack on the United States by an as-yet-unknown enemy. Around the world, people reeled from the news coming over the airwaves and wondered what lay ahead.

The attacks of September 11, 2001, have forever become part of American history. In spite of this, the story of September 11, 2001, is more than

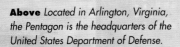

Above Located in Arlington, Virginia, the Pentagon is the headquarters of the United States Department of Defense.

just the tale of one terrible day. It is also the story of how the anti-American sentiment that contributed to the attacks is shared by a small portion of fundamentalist Islamic terror groups that are part of a growing fringe movement. It is the story of the many ways the United States and its allies have responded to the threat of terrorism. It is the story of how the United States – its people and its government – have sought to respond to the attacks, mourn the lost lives and move forward.

Completed in various stages in the early 1970s, the World Trade Center was a group of seven buildings in downtown Manhattan. Hundreds of companies from all over the world rented space in the buildings. The Twin Towers – the North Tower, also called WTC 1, and the South Tower, also called WTC 2 – were the most famous buildings of the group. At 110 stories tall, they stood out among the many tall buildings of the New York City skyline. To some, they were symbols not only of New York City but also of the role of the United States in the international economy. The Twin Towers were home to the offices of banks, insurance companies, investment firms, import-and-export companies, law firms,

technology companies, accounting firms, restaurants, retail businesses, and government agencies.

The terrorists attacked targets that were symbols of the strength of the United States. Foremost among those symbols was the World Trade Center. Less than two hours after the hijacked planes struck them, the Twin Towers collapsed into rubble. The huge hole smashed into the west wall of the Pentagon was a direct attack on the heart of the US armed forces. Investigators believe the terrorists planned to crash the fourth aircraft, which ploughed into the field in Pennsylvania, into either the US Capitol or the White House. If not for efforts of the passengers and crew to regain control of the aircraft, the terrorists probably would have succeeded in hitting all four of their targets.

Above *The west wall of the Pentagon was seriously damaged and 125 people in the building were killed when terrorists crashed American Airlines Flight 77 into it on September 11, 2001.*

Below *United Airlines Flight 175 speeds toward the South Tower of the World Trade Center as the North Tower burns after being hit by American Airlines Flight 11.*

Left *Osama Bin Laden is the head of al-Qaeda, the terrorist group suspected to have been responsible for the attacks of September 11, 2001.*

The perpetrators of the horrific attacks were believed to be members of al-Qaeda. Led by Osama Bin Laden, al-Qaeda attacks people it sees as enemies of Islam. It believes everyone should live under the laws of its extreme version of Islam. Until September 11, most Americans did not know who Bin Laden was, despite the fact that his group had attacked a number of US targets overseas in the past. Soon after the attacks, the faces of Bin Laden and the hijackers were all over the media. So were the faces of their thousands of victims. In the months after the attacks, the *New York Times* ran pictures and short biographies of every victim who died in the hijacked planes, the Twin Towers, and the Pentagon.

In the months following the attacks, the nations of the world rallied to the side of the United States. The United States demanded that Afghanistan, the country that was believed to be sheltering Bin Laden and al-Qaeda, turn over the terrorist leader. When the leaders of Afghanistan refused, the United States and a huge international coalition invaded Afghanistan to capture Bin Laden. As of late 2008, the search for Bin Laden continues.

At about the same time, the fear of terrorism brought about some crises and dramatic changes within the United States itself. Security increased dramatically at nearly every target terrorists might want to attack. Airport security in particular became very tight. Concrete barriers were placed near many tall buildings so that car bombs could not be driven into them. Police guarded important public works, such as dams. The government passed a number of laws it said were needed to fight terrorism. This led to a controversy over whether these new government powers harmed the civil liberties of ordinary Americans. The US government also found itself facing criticism at home and abroad over some of its responses to the attacks, including the decision to send military troops into Iraq in March 2003. To date, no credible evidence has been produced that links Saddam Hussein's regime in Iraq to the attacks of September 11.

In November 2002, the US government set up the National Commission on Terrorist Attacks, also known as the '9/11 Commission'. Commission members studied the events of September 11 to try to tell the story of

Below *Air Force soldiers from Great Britain, the US and Australia work together as part of Operation Iraqi Freedom in 2003.*

what happened during the attacks. In addition, they studied the historic events that led up to the attacks and the question of whether they could have been prevented. Finally, they gave recommendations on how to deal with the threat of terrorism. Their work took almost two years. In July 2004, their final report was released.

In the years since the attacks, every anniversary of them has been marked by mourning and remembrance. A constant stream of books, articles, and editorials discusses the effect of September 11 on the United States and the world, whether the terrorist plot could have been stopped, and how to best prevent future attacks by terrorists. Films have been made about terrorism, the attacks themselves, and the victims. Artists and musicians have also addressed the attacks and their effects. Memorials have been built to make sure the victims will never be forgotten. In 2006, work began on rebuilding the site where the Twin Towers had stood. Freedom Tower, a new and even taller skyscraper, was slowly rising out of the ruins of Ground Zero.

Right The Sphere, a statue by Fritz Koenig, was damaged by the September 11 terrorist attacks. Before the attacks, it stood between the Twin Towers. It now stands in New York City's Battery Park as part of a memorial to the victims of the attacks.

Above *An airport security official checks through passengers' luggage. Following the attacks of 9/11, security checks have become more detailed and time consuming.*

Below *A dramatic pre-September 11 photo of lower Manhattan at dusk. The Twin Towers dwarfed the other buildings in the New York City skyline.*

For air travellers in the eastern United States, the morning of September 11, 2001, looked almost perfect. The sky was clear and cloudless – conditions for air travel could not have been better.

In New York City's World Trade Center, employees began arriving early. About 50,000 people worked in the Twin Towers each day. In addition to these employees, about 40,000 others visited the buildings each day. The visitors included a wide variety of business people, delivery people, and tourists from both near and far who came to look out across New York from the observation decks of the tallest buildings in the city.

The Twin Towers were among the most famous buildings in the United States. From their location in lower Manhattan, they had been the focus of the skyline of New York City since

their completion in the early 1970s. Each tower had 110 stories and stood about 416 metres (1,365 feet) high. Anyone who had ever seen pictures of New York knew what they looked like.

TEAMS OF TERRORISTS

The scene at major airports on the US east coast also looked normal. Passengers checked in, passed through security, and boarded their flights with no sense of danger. Among these flyers, however, were 19 male terrorists. Before the events of September 11, the assumption was that people intending to hijack or blow up a plane would not want to bring harm to themselves – a crucial assumption. Some of the men were pulled aside while going through security and questioned. They were checked with metal-detection wands, or had their bags tested for explosives. Never imagining the terrorists' true purpose, the security officials simply held aside the mens' bags until officials knew the men had boarded their planes. Otherwise, the hijackers simply boarded their flights like ordinary travellers.

At Logan International Airport, in Boston, Massachusetts, five terrorists boarded American Airlines Flight 11,

Above *An airport video camera took this picture of two of the September 11 hijackers before they boarded a plane at Dulles International Airport, in Washington, D.C.*

TIMELINE
1996-2001

1996

Osama Bin Laden moves al-Qaeda from Sudan to Afghanistan.

AUGUST 7, 1998

Al-Qaeda attacks US embassies in Kenya and Tanzania.

AUGUST 20, 1998

The United States fires missiles at an al-Qaeda camp in Afghanistan and a chemical-weapons factory in Sudan.

OCTOBER 12, 2000

Al-Qaeda attacks the USS *Cole.*

JULY 10, 2001

FBI office in Phoenix, Arizona, sends a memo warning of a plot by Osama Bin Laden to train terrorist pilots.

AUGUST 6, 2001

President Bush's daily brief warns 'Bin Laden Determined to Strike in US'.

headed for Los Angeles, California. At about the same time, at another gate in Logan, five more terrorists boarded United Airlines Flight 175, which was also headed for Los Angeles. At Dulles International Airport, located in the suburbs of Washington, D. C., another team of five terrorists took their seats on American Airlines Flight 77. This flight was also bound for Los Angeles. Finally, at Newark International Airport, in New Jersey, four terrorists boarded United Airlines Flight 93, headed for San Francisco, California. Each of the airplanes that the hijackers boarded was a huge passenger jetliner, carrying dozens of travellers. Each airplane was also filled with the thousands of litres of jet fuel needed for a transcontinental flight.

THE NORTH TOWER IS HIT

American Airlines Flight 11 took off just before 8 A.M. The plane was in the air not even 15 minutes when the hijacking began. Flight 11 quickly lost contact with air-traffic controllers,

went off course, and flew into the airspace of another flight. Shortly after the hijacking began, American Airlines received phone calls from flight attendants Betty Ong and Madeline 'Amy' Sweeney describing the hijacking. Two terrorists who were seated in the first-class section, toward the front of the plane, stabbed two flight attendants and forced their way into the cockpit. They quickly turned off the plane's transponder, making it difficult for air-traffic controllers to monitor where the craft was on radar.

"My name is Betty Ong. I'm No. 3 on Flight 11. . . . [T]he cockpit is not answering their phone. There's somebody stabbed in business class, and we can't breathe in business. Um, I think there is some Mace or something. We can't breathe. I don't know, but I think we're getting hijacked. . . . Our No. 1 got stabbed. Our purser is stabbed. Nobody knows who stabbed who. We can't even get up to business class right now because nobody can breathe. . . .(garbled) Our No. 5, our first-class passenger, er, our first-class galley flight attendant and our purser have been stabbed. And we can't get into the cockpit. The door won't open."

Extracts from a phone call from Betty Ong, flight attendant on American Airlines Flight 11 to American Airlines Southeast Reservation Center. As recorded in the FBI transcripts.

"Boston Center: Hey . . . you still there?

New England Region: Yes, I am.

Boston Center: . . . as far as the tape, Bobby seemed to think the guy said that "we have planes." Now, I don't know if it was because it was the accent, or if there's more than one, but I'm gonna, I'm gonna reconfirm that for you, and I'll get back to you real quick. Okay?

New England Region: Appreciate it.

Unidentified Female Voice: They have what?

Boston Center: Planes, as in plural.

Boston Center: It sounds like, we're talking to New York, that there's another one aimed at the World Trade Center.

New England Region: There's another aircraft?

Boston Center: A second one just hit the Trade Center.

New England Region: Okay. Yeah, we gotta get-we gotta alert the military real quick on this."

Conversation between air officials, as transcribed in the 9/11 Commission Report. It took place in the time between the crash of American Flight 11 into the North Tower and the crash of United Flight 175 into the South Tower.

Above *Firefighters, engineers, and FBI agents work at the Pentagon crash site on September 14, 2001.*

Flight 77 as best they could, but with two hijacked planes in the air and a major crisis on their hands, they lost track of it on their radar at about 9:34 A.M. Less than four minutes later, a plane crashed into the Pentagon. Although it was uncertain at the time, within an hour it had been confirmed that the plane that struck the Pentagon was indeed Flight 77.

THE PASSENGERS FIGHT BACK

United Airlines Flight 93 took off late from Newark, New Jersey. It was supposed to take off shortly after 8:00 A.M., but it did not actually leave the ground until 8:42 A.M. – a delay that would prove decisive. By the time Flight 93 was reaching its cruising altitude, air-traffic controllers on the ground knew they were facing a major crisis. At 9:24 A.M., Flight 93 received a warning from United Airlines: "Beware any cockpit intrusion – Two a/c [aircrafts] hit World Trade Center." Two minutes later, the Flight 93 pilot asked his controller to confirm the warning. From the plane, air-traffic controllers then heard one of the pilots yelling, "Mayday! Get out of here! Get out of here! Get out of here!"

Below *The controls of a commercial airliner such as this 747 are very complex. The hijackers had been attending flight schools within the United States to prepare them to fly the planes.*

"Ziad Jarrah: Is that it? Shall we finish it off? Unidentified hijacker: No. Not yet. When they all come, we finish it off."

Excerpt from the cockpit flight recorder onboard Flight 93. The hijackers chose to crash the plane when they realised the passengers were going to break into the cockpit.

RUSHING THE COCKPIT

As on the first two hijacked planes, passengers and crewmembers used air phones and mobile phones to call people on the ground, and reported that the hijackers were stabbing people and threatening the passengers with a bomb. The people on the ground told them that other planes had been hijacked and crashed into buildings. Realising that the terrorists were bluffing about having a bomb – the plane itself was the bomb – the Flight 93 passengers acted quickly. Together, they charged the terrorists. The hijacker pilot, Ziad Jarrah, began flying the plane wildly, trying to stop the passengers from reaching the cockpit. The passengers on Flight 93, however, refused to give up. The plane's flight data recorder captured the sounds of a fierce fight as the passengers struggled with the terrorists to gain entry to the cabin. It also recorded the voices of the terrorists in the cockpit making the decision to crash the plane before the passengers overcame them.

Knowing the likely fate of their flight, the passengers probably knew both that they would not survive, and that they were saving the lives of countless others on the ground. It is not known for certain where the hijackers intended to take Flight 93, however, the most likely targets were either the White House, or the US Capitol building, both in Washington D.C.

TIMELINE
Sept 11, 2001

8:25 A.M.
Flight 11 hijackers broadcast "We have some planes" message.

8:42 A.M.
United Airlines Flight 93 takes off from Newark International Airport, New Jersey.

8:46 A.M.
Flight 11 crashes into the North Tower of the World Trade Center, New York City.

ABOUT 8:47 A.M.
Emergency calls from people in the North Tower reach 911 operators; FDNY calls in more units to help.

Left Memorial for the victims of United Airlines Flight 93, which crashed in a field in Shanksville, Pennsylvania following a struggle between hijackers and passengers.

Below A firefighter pauses while working on the September 11 rescue effort.

some stopped to gather their belongings. A few even tried to keep working. Most people who could get out of the building did just that, in spite of instructions by some 911 operators to wait for help.

DIFFICULT CHOICES

Only about ten minutes after the plane hit the building, the rising smoke and heat were making it unbearable for those trapped above the point of impact in the North Tower. The NYPD considered trying a rooftop helicopter rescue, but the fire and smoke made it impossible. Unable to stand the smoke and heat, many people jumped to their deaths from the burning tower. In other parts of the city, people watching the events through binoculars and telephoto lenses could see people leaping from the building, some of them holding

Above Workers, many of them in shock, flee the burning Twin Towers.

8:57 A.M.
FDNY chiefs give instructions to all officers to evacuate the South Tower.

8:58 A.M.
NYPD orders 1,000 officers to the World Trade Center.

Above *The tops of the Twin Towers of the World Trade Center were engulfed in smoke before the towers collapsed.*

All those aboard the hijacked planes were killed the instant the planes crashed. Not counting the terrorists, 87 people perished on Flight 11; 60 perished on Flight 175; 59 perished on Flight 77; and 40 perished on Flight 93. At the Pentagon, 125 people in the building were killed and 106 more were seriously hurt.

"MORE THAN WE CAN BEAR"
Arriving at a definite number of people killed in the World Trade Center towers has been a more difficult task. When asked to estimate the number of people killed on the day of the attacks, New York Mayor Rudolph Giuliani – no doubt aware of the tens of thousands of people working in and visiting the towers every day – replied that the number was likely to be "more than we can

victims died as a result of all four attacks and crashes. If the numbers given above for the planes and sites in D.C. and Pennsylvania are accurate, then the total figure would include 2,602 people in the Twin Towers.

IN THE NORTH TOWER
Flight 11 hit the North Tower between its 93rd and 99th floors, causing a huge explosion. Not only did the impact and explosion kill everyone in its path,

SEPTEMBER 11

Above *In this view from across the Hudson River in New Jersey, clouds of dust, smoke, and ash rise from the site where the Twin Towers stood.*

radios did not allow them to communicate with each other. However, in spite of the problems they faced, New York City's firefighters, police officers, and other emergency responders did their jobs with great heroism, leading many people to safety.

THE TOWERS FALL
By now, firefighting officials knew that the Twin Towers were severely damaged and that the tops of the building might collapse. The danger of collapse turned out to be far greater than anyone had guessed, however. Just before 10:00 A.M., the South Tower collapsed. With a huge roar, and to the shock of everyone watching from the street or on TV, one of New York's two tallest buildings was gone within ten seconds. As the building fell floor by floor, anyone still inside was undoubtedly killed immediately. The collapsing building blew debris far into the surrounding streets, sending people running for their lives. People in the North Tower heard the roar, but many did not know what had caused it. Fire and police officials rushed to order firefighters and police officers out of the North Tower. About five minutes after the South Tower fell, police officers in helicopters radioed that the top of the North Tower was glowing red, and said they did not think the building would stand for long. As many people as possible got out of the building, but many could not. At 10:28 A.M., the North Tower also collapsed.

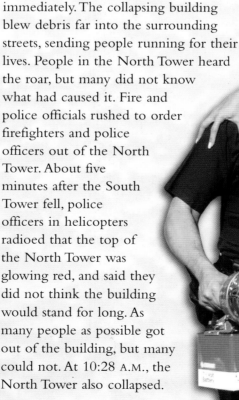

INSIDE THE PENTAGON
American Airlines Flight 77 smashed into the west wall of the Pentagon. The Pentagon is the biggest office building in the United States, but it is only four stories tall. Inside, the Pentagon has five rings of

Above *Firefighters raise the American flag at Ground Zero. For many New Yorkers, this was an important symbol to show that they would not give in to terror.*

Above The attack on the Pentagon left a huge, gaping hole in one side of the building.

TIMELINE
Sept 11, 2001

9:03 A.M.

Flight 175 crashes into the South Tower of the World Trade Center.

9:15 A.M.

FDNY calls in even more firefighters and rescue teams.

9:19 A.M.

United Airlines starts warning all its pilots against the threat of possible cockpit intrusions.

corridors surrounding a courtyard. The giant terrorist bomb that was Flight 77 blasted almost through all of those five rings, but fortunately the damage did not spread through the whole building. Unlike in New York City, police and firefighters in and around Washington, D. C., were prepared to work together in response to an emergency; they had even trained together. Although just as in New York City, nearly every available firefighter and police officer reported for duty, even if they were not rostered to work.

In spite of the great damage to the building, the firefighters and police were able to get the situation under control quickly. Their greatest fear was further attacks. While they were pulling survivors out of the Pentagon, reports came of another hijacked plane headed for Washington. No doubt this was United Flight 93 out of Newark. Thanks to the bravery and sacrifice of the passengers on Flight 93, many lives on the ground were probably saved.

Left Police help a survivor of the World Trade Center attacks.

"I see Officer Smith's face in my mind every day. . . . She was scared, her eyes said as much. But most of all she was courageous. . . .Heroism is not only running into flames. It is doing your job in the face of horror. . . .

'Don't look, keep moving,' she told us; she was shielding you from seeing the destruction. People would have backed up and caused a logjam, she was looking everybody in the eye. No doubt she saw the situation and thought people would stop. She saved hundreds of people.

When I got out of the World Trade Center . . . I called my . . . voice mail and changed the message. 'I am alive,' I said. 'The building has been hit by an airplane.' When I finished the call . . . I saw my building collapse. I knew in my heart Officer Smith was still inside. . . .

I wrote a letter to the [New York Police] Department to make sure they were aware of her heroism. 'There is no doubt,' I wrote, 'that NYPD Officer Smith saved dozens, if not hundreds of lives.'"

Martin Glynn, a computer programmer who worked in the South Tower, remembers Officer Moira Smith, a police officer who saved many lives before being killed in the Tower's collapse.

Above On September 12, 2001, newspaper headlines around the world led with the news of the terrorist attacks on the United States.

When Flight 11 hit the North Tower, many people at first thought it was just a terrible accident. However, as soon as Flight 175 struck the South Tower, and people became aware of the other hijackings, nearly everyone felt the United States was under attack by terrorists.

UNDER ATTACK

Around the country, people were glued to TV, radio, and Internet news sources. Many worried about relatives and friends in New York City and Washington – and about whether more attacks were on the way. To safeguard against future hijackings and attacks, air travel was shut down completely and the financial markets closed. Across the United States and around the world, the headlines of September 12 announced that the United States had been attacked.

Many people felt that the world was about to become a different place. Many people felt that the world had changed forever.

AIR DEFENCE

About 12 minutes after air-traffic controllers in Boston knew that Flight 11 had been hijacked, they alerted officials from NEADS, the Northeast Air Defense Sector. NEADS is part of NORAD, the North American Aerospace Defense Command. NORAD is the federal agency responsible for the defence of US airspace. Less than 10 minutes later, NEADS had scrambled fighter jets from Otis Air Force Base, in Massachusetts, in order to try to intercept the hijacked planes. They were too late. Barely a minute after the fighters took off, Flight 11 hit the North Tower. NEADS did not even know about a second hijacked plane until about the same time Flight 175 hit the South Tower. Other

Below A US Air Force F-16 fighter flies over New York City on September 24, 2003, as part of a NORAD mission.

fighter jets were scrambled from Langley Air Force Base, Virginia, and sent toward Washington, D.C. They did not make it in time to prevent Flight 77 from crashing into the Pentagon. Shortly after authorities realised they were dealing with multiple hijackings, the Federal Aviation Administration (FAA) grounded all flights across the country. No planes were allowed to take off, and all planes in the air were instructed to land as soon as possible. In only a few hours the FAA had landed about 4,500 planes in airports across the country.

THE PRESIDENT SPEAKS

At the time the attacks occurred, President George W. Bush was visiting an elementary school in Sarasota, Florida. While reading with a class of seven year olds in front of an audience of reporters, Bush got the news of airplanes hitting the Twin Towers from an aide. He finished the story and left the classroom for a meeting with his staff. While two hijacked planes were still in the air, Bush held a press conference from the school library. Then, the Secret Service whisked him away into hiding fearing he might be a target for further terrorist attacks. Agents flew him first to Barksdale Air Force Base, in Louisiana, and, then to Offut Air Force Base, near Omaha, Nebraska. Finally – once it seemed clear that the crisis was under control – they flew the president back to Washington. That night, Bush gave a televised speech declaring that the country would stand up to the threat of terrorism.

A NEW ENEMY

In the days after the attacks, the United States struggled to cope with the tragedy and shock. Relatives and friends of people who were in the World Trade Center when it collapsed hung onto fading hopes that their loved ones would be pulled from the wreckage alive, but most were disappointed.

People quickly learned the stories of what happened on the hijacked planes. One detail that stood out – all of the

Left *President George W. Bush gave a televised speech from the Oval Office in the White House on the night of September 11, 2001.*

TIMELINE
Sept 11, 2001

9:37 A.M.

Flight 77 crashes into the Pentagon.

9:58 A.M.

The South Tower of the World Trade Center collapses; FDNY orders firefighters to evacuate North Tower, but some refuse, choosing to stay and help with the rescue effort.

"The pictures of airplanes flying into buildings, fires burning, huge structures collapsing, have filled us with disbelief, terrible sadness, and a quiet, unyielding anger. These acts of mass murder were intended to frighten our nation into chaos and retreat. But they have failed; our country is strong.

A great people has been moved to defend a great nation. Terrorist attacks can shake the foundations of our biggest buildings, but they cannot touch the foundation of America. These acts shattered steel, but they cannot dent the steel of American resolve.

America was targeted for attack because we're the brightest beacon for freedom and opportunity in the world. And no one will keep that light from shining.

Today, our nation saw evil, the very worst of human nature. And we responded with the best of America – with the daring of our rescue workers, with the caring for strangers and neighbors who came to give blood and help in any way they could."

 Excerpt from President Bush's speech on the night of September 11, 2001.

Above *Firefighters and rescue workers remove rubble from the site of the collapsed Twin Towers.*

"On September the 11th, enemies of freedom committed an act of war against our country. Americans have known wars, but for the past 136 years they have been wars on foreign soil, except for one Sunday in 1941. Americans have known the casualties of war, but not at the center of a great city on a peaceful morning . . . . Americans have many questions tonight. Americans are asking, 'Who attacked our country?'

The evidence we have gathered all points to a collection of loosely affiliated terrorist organizations known as al-Qaeda. They are some of the murderers indicted for bombing American embassies in Tanzania and Kenya and responsible for bombing the USS *Cole*. . . .

Our war on terror begins with al-Qaeda, but it does not end there.

It will not end until every terrorist group of global reach has been found, stopped and defeated. "

Excerpts from President Bush's 'War on Terror' speech of September 20, 2001.

terrorists were young, Middle Eastern men. After alert flight attendants reported the terrorists' seat numbers, authorities learned their names. Along with the names and faces of the terrorists, another name and face quickly appeared in the news: Osama Bin Laden. Osama Bin Laden is the leader of al-Qaeda, an Islamist group with a goal of establishing an extremely conservative, fundamentalist brand of Islam as the basis for a world order. An avowed enemy of the United States, al-Qaeda had previously attacked Americans and US targets overseas, and Bin Laden and al-Qaeda quickly became the prime suspects for the September 11 attacks. Two of the hijackers, Khalid al Midhar and Nawaf al Hazmi, turned out to be known members of al-Qaeda. Because of a routine airport mix-up, the luggage of another hijacker, Mohamed Atta, did not make it onto his plane. When authorities opened it following the attacks, they found evidence connecting the hijackings to Islamism. The US government quickly sought to stop further attacks by al-Qaeda.

THE DEPARTMENT OF HOMELAND SECURITY

On September 20, President Bush gave a stirring speech before both houses of the US Congress. He spoke of how the September 11 attacks affected the American people and declared a 'war on terror'. He also discussed how the country would respond to terrorists and their supporters, and how the government would change to help keep Americans safe. One major change he announced was the creation of the Department of Homeland Security. The leader of the new department – former Pennsylvania governor Tom Ridge – would be a member of the president's cabinet. The job of this new department was to organise all of the parts of the government needed to keep the country safe. Its tasks include securing the country's borders, identifying places that are vulnerable to terrorism before they are attacked, responding to emergencies, regulating immigration, and training law enforcement officers.

THE PATRIOT ACT

Another major aspect of the US government's response to the attacks was a new law, the USA Patriot Act, passed on October 26, 2001. This Act gave law enforcement agencies greater powers to watch people suspected of terrorism, search for evidence of crimes, detain suspects who were not US citizens, and share information among themselves. Some Americans worried that the Patriot Act would reduce people's civil liberties by allowing the government to spy on them. In spite of these worries, the government renewed the Patriot Act in March 2006.

FEAR OF MORE ATTACKS

After the attacks of September 11, fears about terrorism became a part of American life. Some of these fears were realistic; others, especially those directed against certain groups of

Above *Urban search-and-rescue teams used dogs to help search for survivors in the mangled wreckage of the Twin Towers.*

TIMELINE
Sept 11, 2001

10:04 A.M.

NYPD helicopter warns that the North Tower roof is glowing red and the top 15 floors look ready to collapse.

10:08 A.M.

Another NYPD helicopter pilot warns that the North Tower looks unstable.

10:24 A.M.

About five FDNY companies return to the North Tower lobby but do not immediately evacuate.

people, were fuelled by ignorance or even prejudice. Knowing that the September 11 terrorists were Muslims, some Americans became suspicious of all Muslims. Although, on a more positive note, many religious and other groups made efforts to increase people's awareness of and sensitivity to fellow Americans who come from a background that is non-Western or non-Christian.

Above *Tom Ridge, the former leader of the US Department of Homeland Security, gives a speech in Washington, D.C., on January 24, 2003.*

"THE LAST NIGHT

Make sure you know all aspects of the plan well, and expect the response, or a reaction, from the enemy. . . .

Check your weapon before you leave and long before you leave. . . .

THE THIRD PHASE

. . . .When the confrontation begins, strike like champions who do not want to go back to this world. Shout, 'Allahu Akbar,' because this strikes fear in the hearts of the non-believers. . . . Know that the gardens of paradise are waiting for you in all their beauty, and the women of paradise are waiting, calling out, 'Come hither, friend of God.' They have dressed in their most beautiful clothing. . . ."

 Excerpts from the document found in Mohamed Atta's luggage giving instructions for the suicide hijacking.

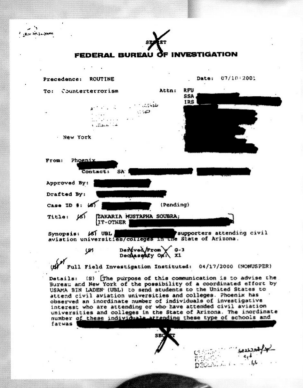

FEDERAL BUREAU OF INVESTIGATION

Precedence: ROUTINE   Date: 07/10/2001

To: Counterterrorism   Attn: RFU
                                  SSA
                                  IRS

New York

From: Phoenix
        Contact: SA
Approved By:
Drafted By:
Case ID #: (U)   (Pending)
Title: (U) ZAKARIA MUSTAPHA SOUBRA;
            IT-OTHER

Synopsis: (U) UBL   supporters attending civil
aviation universities/colleges in the State of Arizona.

(U) Derived From   G-3
      Declassify On   X1

(U) Full Field Investigation Instituted: 04/17/2000 (NONUSPER)

Details: (S) (U) The purpose of this communication is to advise the
Bureau and New York of the possibility of a coordinated effort by
USAMA BIN LADEN (UBL) to send students to the United States to
attend civil aviation universities and colleges. Phoenix has
observed an inordinate number of individuals of investigative
interest who are attending or who have attended civil aviation
universities and colleges in the State of Arizona. The inordinate
number of these individuals attending these type of schools and
fatwas

O sama Bin Laden and al-Qaeda were not known to most Americans until after September 11, 2001. They were quite well known, however, to US government leaders and members of the intelligence community. In July 2001, FBI agents in Phoenix, Arizona, sent a memo (now known as the 'Phoenix Memo') warning of Bin Laden supporters taking flying classes in Arizona. Little more than one month before the attacks, the Presidential Daily Brief included the warning 'Bin Laden Determined to Strike in US.'

Above The 'Phoenix Memo' shows that the FBI suspected al-Qaeda might try to use airplanes in a terrorist attack.

AL-QAEDA HISTORY

Al-Qaeda got its start in Afghanistan in the late 1980s. From 1979 to 1988, the Soviet Union had invaded Afghanistan and was attempting to set-up a pro-Soviet government. The battle in Afghanistan drew thousands of Islamist fighters, called 'mujahideen', from around the world to fight a 'jihad', or struggle, against the Soviet giant. It was the time of the Cold War, a period of intense rivalry between the United States and the Soviet Union.

The United States gave millions of dollars and weapons to help fight this attempted Soviet expansion. One of the Islamists who went to fight in Afghanistan was Osama Bin Laden. A son of one of the wealthiest families in Saudi Arabia, Bin Laden became an important figure in the struggle against the Soviet Union through his financial donations to the cause. He also helped create an organisation that brought Islamist fighters to Afghanistan. By the time the Soviet Union finally pulled out of Afghanistan, Bin Laden had made his name as the leader of an Islamist group called al-Qaeda, or 'the base'. He had also made contacts with other Islamist leaders, including Ayman al-Zawahiri, who was a major figure in a group called Egyptian Islamic Jihad.

Left An early picture of a smiling Osama Bin Laden sitting in a cave in Afghanistan (1988).

Above *Mujahideen fighters in Afghanistan battled the Soviet Union in the 1980s.*

TIMELINE 2001

SEPTEMBER 21, 2001

'America: A Tribute to Heroes' airs.

SEPTEMBER – NOVEMBER 2001

Letters containing deadly anthrax spores are sent to news media offices and to two democratic US senators, killing five people and infecting 17 others.

OCTOBER 7, 2001

Operation Enduring Freedom – the invasion designed to find Osama Bin Laden and eradicate al-Qaeda – begins as the United States launches air strikes and raids in Afghanistan.

THE GULF WAR

In 1990, Bin Laden began moving al-Qaeda to Sudan, where an Islamic government was growing in power. He himself moved back to Saudi Arabia. Later that year, Saudi Arabia's neighbour, Iraq, invaded the small, oil-rich nation of Kuwait and threatened the whole region. Bin Laden suggested that the Saudi government use al-Qaeda to fight Iraq, but the Saudis turned him down. The Saudi government instead allowed the United States and other Western nations to base their forces in Saudi Arabia while fighting Iraq. The idea of non-Muslims fighting in Saudi Arabia enraged Bin Laden. He became an enemy of his own country and fled to Sudan.

Above *A tank rides through the Afghan streets during the Soviet invasion of Afghanistan.*

"As more recruits were trained in Afghanistan during the late 1990s, so ever more terrorist attacks were prepared. In the aftermath of the 1998 US embassy bombings, men controlled or encouraged by Osama bin Laden were responsible for planning an array horrendous atrocities. Cells plotted to kill President Bush, destroy . . . . US embassies in New Delhi, Paris, and Albania, and launch a multi-continent attack . . . . An attack was also plotted on a nuclear reactor in Sydney, Australia, during the 2000 Olympic Games, and plans were discovered for a gas attack in London, almost certainly on the subway system."

Simon Reeve was the first to write a book about Osama Bin Laden and al-Qaeda, The New Jackals. First published in 1998, it was updated after the events of 9/11 with new material warning of further attacks against Western targets by al-Qaeda.

Above *A Norwegian commercial lift ship brings the USS Cole back to the United States for repairs after it was attacked by al-Qaeda.*

dictatorship governed by their very strict version of Islam. Bin Laden built al-Qaeda training camps in Afghanistan, and used that nation as a base for numerous terrorist plots.

ATTACKS ON US EMBASSIES

In February 1998, he issued a religious order, called a 'fatwa', declaring that Muslims had a duty to kill Americans. About six months later, on August 7, 1998, al-Qaeda members drove trucks loaded with bombs into the US embassies in two African cities – Nairobi, Kenya, and Dar es Salaam, Tanzania. In Nairobi, 213

GROWING IN STRENGTH

In Sudan, he built al-Qaeda into a powerful and dangerous group. Its goal was promote Islamic government and to fight anyone who stood in its way. His main enemy became the United States, which he said was the 'head of the snake' that oppressed Muslims. In addition to his opposition to the United States stationing non-Muslim armies in Muslim lands, he also opposed the United States for supporting Israel – which militant Islamists see as an enemy nation.

THE TALIBAN

By 1996, the government of Sudan had turned against him. However, luckily for Bin Laden, the new Islamic government of Afghanistan, a group called the Taliban, welcomed him and al-Qaeda. The Taliban started out as a movement of students but by 1996, they had turned Afghanistan into a

Below *Zacarias Moussaoui was arrested in the United States for having an expired visa after his flight instructor reported him to the FBI as a possible terrorist.*

Right *Ayman al-Zawahiri is al-Qaeda's second-in-command leader.*

people were killed, including 12 Americans, and about 5,000 were injured. In Dar es Salaam, 11 people were killed. Al-Qaeda faxed messages to London taking responsibility for the attacks. The United States responded, a few weeks later, by shooting missiles at an al-Qaeda training camp in Afghanistan and a chemical-weapons plant in Sudan, but failed to kill Bin Laden. In October 2000, al-Qaeda struck again. Using a small boat filled with explosives, al-Qaeda suicide bombers blew a hole in the side of the USS *Cole*, killing 17 and injuring 47.

RUNNING OUT OF TIME

Throughout the US government, officials knew that al-Qaeda was a serious threat to Americans. US intelligence agencies heard from sources that a major attack was planned, but they did not know details. Some even suspected an attack on US soil. They did not know how quickly time was running out. A few months after the USS *Cole* attack in October 2000, all of the al-Qaeda terrorists who would pilot planes on September 11 were already in the United States

taking flying lessons. During late 2000 and early 2001, the remaining hijackers got visas to enter the United States, and spent time at al-Qaeda training camps in Afghanistan. By July 2001, they were all in the United States, making the last preparations for the attack.

MISSED OPPORTUNITIES

Most of the terrorists were not known to US law enforcement and intelligence agencies. While preparing for the attacks, they tried not to draw attention to themselves. Two of the terrorists, however, were known members of al-Qaeda. The Federal Bureau of Investigation (FBI) and the Central Intelligence Agency (CIA) believed that Khalid al-Midhar and Nawaf al-Hazmi were involved in the *Cole* bombing. Even though worried by having terrorists loose in the United States, the FBI and the CIA could not agree on how to handle the case of Midhar and Hazmi and did not take action

OCTOBER 20, 2001

'The Concert for New York City' takes place in Madison Square Garden.

Above The seal of the FBI.

"7 August 2001: the FBI does not recognize the significance of the information regarding al-Mihdhar and al-Hazmi's possible arrival in the United States and thus does not take adequate action to share information, assign resources, and give sufficient priority to the search.

8 August 2001: FBI headquarters does not recognize the significance of the information regarding Moussaoui's training and beliefs and thus does not take adequate action to share information, involve higher-level officials across agencies, obtain information regarding Moussaoui's ties to al Qaeda, and give sufficient priority to determining what Moussaoui might be planning.

10 August 2001: the CIA and FBI do not connect the presence of al-Mihdhar, al-Hazmi, and Moussaoui to the general threat reporting about imminent attacks."

Missed opportunities by the CIA to use, or to communicate, information gathered on the hijackers in the United States during the months before the attacks as documented in the report of the 9/11 Commission.

Above Firefighters respond to the al-Qaeda bombing of the US embassy in Nairobi, Kenya.

Above *US Special Forces soldiers pose for a picture with members of the Northern Alliance, allies in the fight against the Taliban. The American soldiers' faces have been blurred to protect their identities.*

to find them. In another case, a civilian flight instructor suspected one of his students, Zacarias Moussaoui, might be a terrorist and reported him to the FBI. Finding that Moussaoui was in the United States illegally, the FBI arrested him in August 2001 but did not search his belongings. It was not until after the attacks that they discovered he too was connected to al-Qaeda. No one knows whether better intelligence work could have stopped the attacks of September 11, 2001. It is possible, however, that connecting al-Qaeda members in the United States to the idea of using airplanes as giant bombs could have saved thousands of lives.

AFTER THE ATTACKS

After the attacks of September 11, 2001, the US government was jolted into action. Other nations such as Britain, Spain and Australia rushed to support the United States. President Bush demanded that the Taliban turn over Bin Laden and other al-Qaeda leaders to face trial. When they refused, the United States put together a coalition of allies and invaded Afghanistan. The coalition found support even in Afghanistan. The Northern Alliance, an Afghan rebel group that opposed the Taliban, worked with the international coalition to defeat the Taliban. The coalition quickly toppled the Taliban from power. Finding Bin Laden and the other al-Qaeda leaders proved harder. In one fierce battle at the network

"[W]e calculated in advance the number of casualties from the enemy, who would be killed based on the position of the tower. We calculated that the floors that would be hit would be three or four floors. I was the most optimistic of them all . . . . due to my experience in this field, I was thinking that the fire from the gas in the plane would melt the iron structure of the building and collapse the area where the plane hit and all the floors above it only. This is all that we had hoped for. . . . We had notification since the previous Thursday that the event would take place that day. We had finished our work that day and had the radio on. It was 5:30 P.M. our time. . . . Immediately, we heard the news that a plane had hit the World Trade Center. We turned the radio station to the news from Washington. The news continued and no mention of the attack until the end. At the end of the newscast, they reported that a plane just hit the World Trade Center."

Excerpt from the transcript of a video in which Osama Bin Laden discusses the 9/11 attacks. The video was broadcast in the US on December 13, 2001.

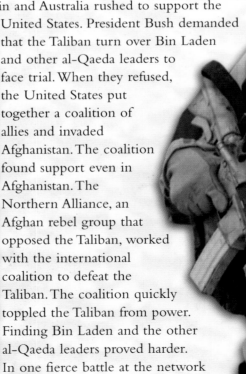

🎞 **FILM EXCERPT**   🗄 **DOCUMENT**   🎙 **INTERVIEW/BOOK EXTRACT**   🎵 **SONG/POEM**

Above US newspaper headlines following the July 7, 2005 bombings in London. Four Islamist suicide bombers detonated bombs on underground trains and buses killing 52 people and injuring hundreds. One of the bombers recorded a video statement in which he warned of further attacks if British troops were not withdrawn from Iraq and Afghanistan.

of caves known as Tora Bora, coalition forces thought they had a good chance of catching or killing the al-Qaeda leader, but he got away. After the battle, the United States military was criticised for giving too much responsibility in the fight to the Northern Alliance rather than using its own highly trained soldiers.

ATTACKS AROUND THE WORLD

Al-Qaeda has been linked to a number of terrorist bombings targeting countries other than the United States. On March 11, 2004, four packed commuter trains in Madrid were ripped apart by bombs killing 192 people and injuring hundreds. The bombers claimed to have been inspired by al-Qaeda. There have also been lucky escapes – an attempted bombing of London underground trains and buses on July 21, 2005 was narrowly avoided when the detonators failed to ignite the explosives.

AL-QAEDA TODAY

Although there was a new democratically elected government in Afghanistan, the country continued to struggle. In mid 2008, there were reports that the Taliban was regaining strength. In the years following the WTC attacks, al-Qaeda had continued to carry out terrorist attacks – including the March 11, 2004, attacks in Madrid, and the July 7, 2005, attacks in London – and Bin Laden remained at large.

Left A US Special Forces soldier stands guard for a US official visiting Afghanistan in November 2001.

TIMELINE 2001-2002

OCTOBER 26, 2001
Congress passes USA Patriot Act.

DECEMBER 18, 2001
Congress passes resolution declaring September 11 now to be known as 'Patriot Day.'

DECEMBER 22, 2001
American Airlines passengers foil British-born 'shoebomber,' Richard Reid.

2002
Marvel Comics releases a special issue of The Amazing Spider-Man.

MARCH 2002
Jules and Gedeon Naudet's 9/11 is shown on TV.

MARCH 11, 2002
'Tribute in Light' first appears six months after the attacks.

MAY 8, 2002
Jose Padilla, a US citizen is arrested under suspicion of plotting a radioactive 'dirty bomb' attack.

JULY 4, 2002
Toby Keith's Courtesy of the Red, White, and Blue (The Angry American) is #1 on US Billboard's country singles chart.

AUGUST 17, 2002
Bruce Springsteen's The Rising goes to #1 on the US Billboard 200 chart.

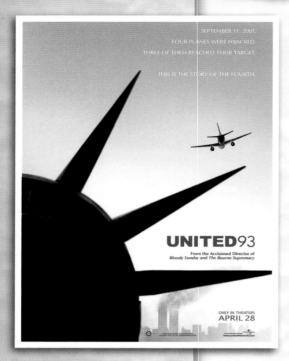

SEPTEMBER 11, 2001.
FOUR PLANES WERE HIJACKED.
THREE OF THEM REACHED THEIR TARGET.

THIS IS THE STORY OF THE FOURTH.

UNITED93

From the Acclaimed Director of
Bloody Sunday and *The Bourne Supremacy*

ONLY IN THEATERS
APRIL 28

Above *This poster advertises the film United 93, a re-enactment of the dramatic events over Pennsylvania that was released in 2006.*

"New York City has traditionally served as the backdrop for many comic books that have entertained readers for decades. Not coincidentally, many comic book publishers-including Marvel-have also made their home in our City. I think we all now realize that we do not have to read fiction to find examples of heroism. The real heroes in American life have been with us all along. Our firefighters, police officers, and other rescue workers put their lives on the line every day to protect the rest of us from danger."

Former New York City Mayor Rudolph Giuliani, in the foreword to Marvel Comics' A Moment of Silence *special edition.*

voices reading the names of the September 11 victims, along with an orchestra and chorus. The piece was first performed by the New York Philharmonic in 2002. In 2003, it won the Pulitzer Prize for music.

LITERATURE AND COMICS

Hundreds of books have been published about September 11. Non-fiction books have looked at everything from the events leading up to the attacks, to government responses, to the stories of survivors and witnesses. Famous fiction writers, including John Updike, Jonathan Safran Foer, and Martin Amis, have also set stories in the days after the attacks. A special issue of the Amazing Spider-Man series imagined the reaction to the attacks from superhero characters and paid tribute to the firefighters and other rescue workers who dealt with the tragedy in real life. Comic book companies, including Marvel and DC Comics, produced special editions in which their illustrators showed scenes of the rescuers at work and donated the profits to charity.

Pulitzer Prize-winning graphic artist Art Spiegelman wrote a comic-style book about September 11 entitled *In the Shadow of No Towers*. In this work, Spiegelman takes an intensely personal approach to the attacks, admitting the traumatic effect the attacks had on

Right *A scene from a special edition comic called Heroes published by Marvel Comics, which honours the firemen involved in September 11.*

him as a New Yorker, an artist, a parent, and an American. He also uses his art and his writing to lament the tragic events of September 11, and the subsequent changes brought about as a result of the attacks.

ON THE BIG SCREEN

In September of 2001, French filmmakers Jules and Gedeon Naudet were working on a documentary about New York City firefighters. While riding with the firefighters on the morning of September 11, Jules heard a low-flying plane and began filming it just before it smashed into the North Tower. As the firefighters responded to the attacks on the World Trade Center, he kept filming. The Naudets' film turned into a documentary about New York firefighters on the day of the attacks. Titled *9/11*, it was shown on TV in March 2002, only six months after the attacks. Also in 2002, French producer Alain Brigand came out with *11'09"01*, or *September 11*. For this film, Brigand commissioned 11

Above World Trade Center *star Nicolas Cage holds a press conference on September 12, 2006, to discuss the opening of his film based on the attack on the Twin Towers.*

filmmakers from around the world to make short films – each 11 minutes, 9 seconds, and 1 frame long – that express views of the attacks.

About five years after the attacks, Hollywood began releasing films about the tragic events of September 11. *United 93* (2006) and *Flight 93* (2006) explored the drama of the plane that crashed in a Pennsylvania field when the passengers fought the terrorists. *World Trade Center* (2006) starred Nicolas Cage as real-life Port Authority police sergeant, John McLoughlin, who survived the collapse of the South Tower. Other films used fictional characters to explore the effects of the attacks on individuals. *Reign Over Me* (2007) starred Adam Sandler as a man devastated by the loss of his family in one of the hijacked planes. *The Great New Wonderful* (2005) looked at the effect of the attacks on New Yorkers one year after they occurred. In the film, the characters struggle with the memory of the tragedy without ever mentioning it.

FINE ARTS

On September 11, the collapse of the Twin Towers destroyed a 70-year-old tree that grew nearby. Even as it was broken, the tree shielded St. Paul's Chapel, one of the oldest buildings in the city, from harm. Sculptor Steve Tobin created a bronze recreation of the tree, called Trinity Root, that was installed at the corner of Wall Street and Broadway, near Ground Zero, on September 11, 2005. In 2002, the Metropolitan Museum of Art in New York held an exhibit of photography called 'Life of the City' that concluded with monitors showing a constantly changing stream of pictures showing the events of September 11.

Above Trinity Root *is a sculpture that was modelled from the roots of the tree that protected St. Paul's Chapel on September 11, 2001.*

TIMELINE 2005-2011

JUNE 2005
Freedom Tower design is released.

SEPTEMBER 7, 2005
Flight 93 Memorial plan is announced.

SEPTEMBER 11, 2008
The memorial park at the Pentagon opens.

2011
National September 11 Memorial and Museum at the World Trade Center planned to open in time for tenth anniversary of attacks.

"It was a priority for us to show the families of the firemen the truth at the World Trade Center – those 73 firemen who had died on that morning. It was very important for us to show to their families this footage before anybody would see it, before it would be aired on television. And it was a very long and hard process to recognize everybody on Jules' footage but we finally got all the names together and contacted the families and then sent them a tape and they all thanked us because in a way it was seeing their loved one before the last moment. But not panicking, not in fear, but doing this job that they always loved to do- with this face of courage and I believe it made those families feel a bit better."

Filmmaker Gedeon Naudet talking about showing 9/11 to the families of NYC firefighters who were killed on September 11.

"Timeless in simplicity and beauty,
like its landscape, both stark and serene,
the Memorial should be quiet in reverence,
yet powerful in form,
a place both solemn and uplifting.

It should instill pride, and humility.
The Memorial should offer intimate experience,
yet be heroic in scale.
Its strong framework should be open to natural change
and allow freedom of personal interpretation.

We want to restore life here,
to heal the land, and nourish our souls.
In this place, a scrap yard will become a gateway
and a strip mine will grow into a flowering meadow

But more than restoring health,
the Memorial should be radiant,
in loving memory of the passengers and crew
who gave their lives on Flight 93."

**Memorial Expression
by Paul and Milena Murdoch,
Flight 93 National Memorial Architects.**

*A*fter the attacks of September 11, 2001, Americans showed both their sorrow and their patriotism. Many people displayed American flags on their houses, wore memorial ribbons and put American flags and memorial bumper stickers on their cars. The attacks came to be known simply as '9/11', and the site where the Twin Towers once stood became known as 'Ground Zero'. All that was left where the Twin Towers stood was a deep crater.

Above
Many people have worn stars-and-stripes ribbons to signify patriotism and remembrance of the victims of the attacks of September 11.

MEMORIALS

After the attacks, people began using the fence around St. Paul's Chapel, which stands near Ground Zero, as a memorial wall. Family members and friends of those who died in the attacks posted pictures and tributes to their loved ones.

Below *"Tribute in Light", in which twin beams of light take the place of the Twin Towers, shines up from Ground Zero on September 11 each year.*

Many people – New Yorkers and those visiting the city – spent time at the fence reading the tributes. Six months after the attacks, New York City remembered the Twin Towers by shining 88 powerful beams of light upward from Ground Zero. The display was called 'Tribute in Light'. It appeared again on September 11, 2002, and it has also appeared every September 11 since then. In early January 2004, a design by architects Michael Arad and Peter Walker won a competition for the National September 11 Memorial and Museum at the World Trade Center. The memorial will take up 33,000 square metres, and it will include pools

of water into which will flow the largest manmade waterfalls in the United States. Construction began on this memorial in May 2006. It is projected to open in 2011.

At the Pentagon, a memorial park scheduled to open in September 2008 features 184 individual memorial units – 125 representing people killed in the Pentagon and 59 for those killed aboard Flight 77. The National Parks Service runs Flight 93 National Memorial in Pennsylvania. The memorial features 40 large wind chimes and 40 memorial maple groves – one for each victim – as well as ponds and a Field of Honor that marks the crash site.

Above *Memorial in New York City for loved ones who died in the Twin Towers.*

YEARLY REMEMBRANCE
On December 18, 2001, the United States Congress passed a resolution saying that each September 11 in the future would be observed as Patriot Day. On the first anniversary of the attacks, President Bush met at Ground Zero with families that lost members in the attacks. People in New York held candlelight vigils around the city. New York City Mayor Michael Bloomberg dedicated an eternal memorial light in Battery Park to the victims of the attacks.

STILL STRUGGLING
Recovery from the attacks and remembrance of those lost has become a part of American life. In spite of all the response, recovery, and memorial efforts, however, studies in 2005 and 2006 showed that many survivors of

". . . . On Patriot Day, we remember the innocent victims, and we pay tribute to the valiant firefighters, police officers, emergency personnel, and ordinary citizens who risked their lives so others might live.

. . . . All Americans honor the selfless men and women of our Armed Forces, the dedicated members of our public safety, law enforcement, and intelligence communities, and the thousands of others who work hard each day to protect our country, secure our liberty, and prevent future attacks.

The spirit of our people is the source of America's strength, and 6 years ago, Americans came to the aid of neighbors in need. On Patriot Day, we pray for those who died and for their families. We volunteer to help others and demonstrate the continuing compassion of our citizens. On this solemn occasion, we rededicate ourselves to laying the foundation of peace with confidence in our mission and our free way of life."

Proclamation from President George W. Bush on Patriot Day, 2007.

September 11, 2001 A Timeline

Left *Visitors to Ground Zero gather to read through the tributes and information at the site.*

Above *A memorial service for the victims of the September 11 terrorist attacks, held at Ground Zero.*

the attacks were still deeply traumatised. Organisations such as the World Trade Center Survivors Network help survivors cope with the aftermath of the attacks by providing peer support and counselling services. The group has also worked to help preserve the Survivor's Stairway. Many survivors of the attacks escaped the North Tower by this stairway, and it was the last piece of the Twin Towers left standing in its original place. The Survivors' Stairway was relocated to the National September 11 Memorial and Museum at the World Trade Center where it will be on display.

Above *An artist's conception shows what the New York City skyline will look like after Freedom Tower is completed.*

SEPTEMBER 11 AND US POLITICS

The attacks of September 11, 2001, have left a deep mark on politics in the United States. So too has the war in Iraq that was launched in part on the belief that Iraq was harbouring weapons of mass destruction that might be used in future terrorist attacks. In the 2004 election, incumbent Republican candidate, George W. Bush and Democratic challenger, John Kerry presented different ideas about how to best keep Americans safe from terrorism and how to prevent attacks.

As the 2008 presidential election approached, how the United States should deal with the threat of terrorism was again a major topic.

"I was driving to a state legislative hearing in downtown Chicago when I heard the news on my car radio: a plane had hit the World Trade Center. By the time I got to my meeting, the second plane had hit, and we were told to evacuate.

People gathered in the streets and looked up at the sky and the Sears Tower, transformed from a workplace to a target. We feared for our families and our country. We mourned the terrible loss suffered by our fellow citizens. Back at my law office, I watched the images from New York: a plane vanishing into glass and steel; men and women clinging to windowsills, then letting go; tall towers crumbling to dust. It seemed all of the misery and all of the evil in the world were in that rolling black cloud, blocking out the September sun.

What we saw that morning forced us to recognize that in a new world of threats, we are no longer protected by our own power. And what we saw that morning was a challenge to a new generation."

Excerpt from a speech by presidential candidate, Barack Obama, August 1, 2007.

In 2007, Illinois senator (and 2008 presidential candidate) Barack Obama talked about his memories of September 11, 2001, when he was a lawyer working in Chicago.

In early 2008, one of the first candidates for the Republican presidential nomination was Rudolph Giuliani, who had been mayor of New York City at the time of the attacks. When Giuliani withdrew, he gave his support to Arizona Senator John McCain. In May 2008, McCain gave a speech which talked about what he thought he could achieve if elected president. Among his main goals were fighting al-Qaeda and preventing terrorism in the US.

FREEDOM TOWER

After September 11, 2001, many people wondered whether the Twin Towers would ever be rebuilt. Some thought it was too dangerous to again build such huge skyscrapers. Others thought that not to rebuild would send the message to the terrorists that they had won. By 2003, plans were in place to build a new group of buildings on the World Trade Center site. The centrepiece would be the 541-metre-tall Freedom Tower. Construction on Freedom Tower began in 2006. It is due to be finished in 2012. By mid 2008, people at street level could see the steel supports for the new building as they began reaching above the lip of the crater. All those who died in the Twin Towers will always be remembered in Freedom Tower. On some of the steel supports close to the building's foundation, family members of many of the people who perished on September 11, 2001 have written messages to their loved ones.

Above This aerial view of the future World Trade Center Memorial and Museum was created by an artist. The waterfalls will be in the 'footprints' of the original World Tade Center Towers.

Left Family members of victims write messages on a steel beam forming part of the base of Freedom Tower.

RAMZI BINALSHIBH (1972-)

Ramzi Binalshibh was originally supposed to be one of the al-Qaeda terrorist pilots in the attacks of September 11, 2001. He was a friend and roommate of Mohamed Atta in Hamburg, Germany. After he was repeatedly denied entry into the United States because of concerns over the possibility that he might become involved in terrorist activities, Binalshibh continued working on the planning and financing of the attacks. He was arrested after a huge gunfight in Karachi, Pakistan, on September 11, 2002, one year to the day after the attacks on the WTC. Binalshibh is also believed to have been involved with the al-Qaeda attack on the USS *Cole* in 2000. As of 2008, he was a prisoner at the US military base in Guantanamo Bay, Cuba.

OSAMA BIN LADEN (1957-)

Osama Bin Laden comes from one of Saudi Arabia's richest families. In about 1980, he went to Afghanistan to fight the Soviet Union. He used his wealth to fund recruitment and training of fighters and met Ayman al-Zawahiri. There the two joined their groups into al-Qaeda, a larger militant Islamist group. Bin Laden is especially hostile toward the United States, having called on Muslims to kill Americans. Al-Qaeda has organised many acts of terrorism, including the September 11 attacks. Since the invasion of Afghanistan following September 11, he has been one of the most wanted men in the world. Many believe he is hiding in the mountains between Afghanistan and Pakistan; some think he may already be dead.

AYMAN AL-ZAWAHIRI (1951-)

Ayman al-Zawahiri was born in Egypt and educated as a doctor. At a young age, Zawahiri became an Islamist. He joined the Muslim Brotherhood as a teenager and went on to become a major leader of Egyptian Islamic Jihad. In the 1980s, Zawahiri was arrested and jailed in connection with the assassination of Egyptian president, Anwar al-Sadat. By the late 1980s, he had joined forces with Bin Laden and also become Bin Laden's personal physician. He is said to be al-Qaeda's second-in-command and one of the group's top strategists. Along with Bin Laden, Zawahiri is one of the world's most wanted terrorists. In 2006, the United States fired a missile at a target in Pakistan in an attempt to kill Zawahiri, but missed.

MOHAMMED OMAR (1959-)

Mullah Mohammed Omar is the leader of the Taliban, the Islamist group that ruled Afghanistan from 1996 to late 2001. Little is known about his life except that he is missing one eye. Omar fought the Soviet Union when it tried to take over Afghanistan in the 1980s. After the Soviets' defeat, he led a student movement – the Taliban – to control of Afghanistan in 1996. Under his leadership, the Taliban put in place a harsh version of Islamic law. Also in 1996, Omar's government allowed al-Qaeda to base its terrorist training camps in Afghanistan. Following the September 11 attacks, Omar refused to hand Bin Laden and other al-Qaeda leaders over for trial. Since the 2001 invasion of Afghanistan, Omar has been in hiding.

MOHAMED ATTA (1968-2001)

Mohamed Atta piloted American Airlines Flight 11 into the North Tower of the World Trade Center and is believed to have been the leader of the September 11 hijackers. Born in Egypt, Atta is said to have been a serious, religious, and studious young man. In the mid 1990s, he was a student in Hamburg, Germany, when he grew increasingly angry and radical. It is not known exactly when he joined al-Qaeda, but in Hamburg, he became close with other young men who shared his views, including two others who also suicide-piloted planes on September 11. In 2000, Atta arrived in the United States to take flying lessons and prepare for the attacks.

KHALID SHAIKH MOHAMMED (1965-)

Khalid Shaikh Mohammed was a wanted terrorist long before he joined al-Qaeda in 1998. In the mid 1990s, he worked with Ramzi Yousef – the main terrorist responsible for the 1993 World Trade Center bombing and his nephew – on plots to assassinate President Bill Clinton and blow up commercial airplanes. While on the run from US authorities, he joined al-Qaeda. Mohammed was captured in Pakistan in 2003. Until 2006, he was held in secret CIA prisons. That year, he was moved to a US prison in Guantanamo Bay, Cuba. At a 2006 hearing, Mohammed confessed to planning the September 11 attacks.

GLOSSARY

9/11 Commission The popular name for the National Commission on Terrorist Attacks Upon the United States. Its purpose was to compile a complete record of the events of September 11, as well as to make recommendations to prevent future terrorist attacks upon the United States. Its findings were released in 2004.

Air-traffic controller A person who tells pilots when it is safe to take off and land, and also monitors the routes of planes to prevent accidents.

Allies People or countries that cooperate with each other. It is often used to refer to countries that take military action together.

al-Qaeda The Islamist group led by Osama Bin Laden held responsible for the terrorist attacks of September 11, 2001, and many other acts of terrorism throughout the world. Its name means 'the base' in Arabic.

Anthrax A type of bacteria that causes a deadly disease that attacks the lungs and skin.

Beacon A device on an aircraft that gives out a signal that helps air-traffic controllers guide the craft.

Bioterrorism Attacking people with germs, such as anthrax, to cause disease or death.

Bureaucratic Following a set of rules or procedures, especially within a large organisation or government office.

Cabinet A group of leaders of government agencies that advise the president or prime minister of a country.

Chemical weapons Weapons designed to harm people with chemicals, such as gases which damage or irritate the skin, or are breathed in.

Civil liberties The freedoms, such as those guaranteed by the US Bill of Rights, that restrict the government from controlling or interfering in individuals' lives.

Civil war A war between different groups within the same country.

Coalition A group that agrees to work and act together to achieve the same agreed goal or outcome.

Cold War The period of political hostility between the United States and the Soviet Union after World War II in which the two superpowers competed for power by supporting and arming other countries.

Command A base from which leaders – military or political – give orders.

Communist A person who believes in a classless society in which the state controls wealth and ownership.

Controversy Disagreement over an idea.

Dictatorship A form of government in which a single ruler has total power over the rule of a country. Dictators usually gain this power through violence.

Dirty bomb A terrorist weapon that spreads radioactive material through an explosion. It is not the same as a nuclear bomb which can spread radioactive material for hundreds of kilometres. Any radiation spread by a dirty bomb would only cover a few kilometres of the explosion.

Embassy A building in one country that is the headquarters of the ambassador from a foreign country.

Evacuation The process of getting people out of a building or an area, usually when there is great danger.

Fatwa A ruling on a point of Islamic law by a recognised religious authority.

Financial markets Institutions for the trade of stocks and bonds.

Grounded Forced or restricted to stay in a certain area.

Hijack To take control of a vehicle, such as an airplane or boat, by force and often for political purposes. Most hijackings aim to make the plane land somewhere other than its intended destination.

Immigration Coming to live in a new country.

Intelligence Information gathered about enemy activity.

Intercept To stop something before it reaches its target.

Intrusion The act of forcing oneself into a restricted area.

Islamist A person who thinks government should be controlled by the laws of Islam.

Jihad In Islam, it means a struggle brought about by religious duty.

Mace A chemical spray that disables people for a short time. It causes intense pain and discomfort to the eyes, and can also cause the victim trouble breathing. The effects can last between 30 minutes and 2 hours.

Mayday The international distress call used by planes and ships.

Mujahideen Islamic guerilla fighters.

NATO A political and military alliance formed after World War II that includes Great Britain, the United States and other European allies.

Northern Alliance The name given to the remaining members of the Afghan regime which held power until 1995, when the Taliban took over.

Pepper spray A spray that uses pepper to temporarily disable people by irritating the eyes, nose, throat and skin. It was used by the hijackers to disable the passengers and prevent them being able to fight back.

Press conference A gathering of reporters to hear a speech by a public figure. The press can usually ask questions after the speech.

Public address system A system of speakers placed throughout a building so people can hear announcements. They are usually used for fire drills or safety announcements.

Pulitzer Prize A prize given in the United States for achievements in literature, journalism, or music, funded by the estate of Joseph Pulitzer.

Radar A system that uses radio waves to tell the locations of faraway objects. It is used to determine the speed, size and location of ships and planes.

Resolution A document expressing the official view of a group or government.

Secret Service A government agency that protects the president and other top officials.

Soviet Union The former communist country made up of Russia and fourteen other republics that existed between 1922 and 1991.

Taliban The name literally means 'students of Islamic knowledge'. Leaders of this political movement took over Afghanistan in 1996 and imposed a strict form of Islamic rule. They were removed from power in 2001 after a co-operative operation between the Northern Alliance and NATO.

Telethon A long television programme used to raise money for a particular cause.

Terrorists People who use random or planned acts of violence to scare others into giving in to their political or financial demands.

Transcontinental Travelling across a continent.

Transponder A device in a plane that responds to radar by sending back a radio signal with identifying information.

Traumatised Deeply upset by injury or emotional stress.

Vigil A peaceful demonstration, often at night, where candles are lit and speeches or prayers may be said. They are often held in remembrance of a person or an event.

Weapons of mass destruction Weapons designed to kill large numbers of people at one time, including biological, chemical, and nuclear weapons.

World Trade Center The complex of seven buildings in Manhattan that included the Twin Towers. All were destroyed in the attacks of September 11.

INDEX

ACKNOWLEDGMENTS

PICTURE CREDITS:

Every effort has been made to trace the copyright holders, and we apologise in advance for any unintentional ommissions. We would be pleased to insert the appropriate acknowledgements in any subsequent edition of this publication.

B=bottom; C=centre; L=left; R=right; T=top

Sean Adair/Corbis: 5b, 11. AFP/Getty Images: OFCtl. AP/PA Photos: 43tl. Robert F. Bukaty/AFP/Getty Images: 15t. Central Intelligence Agency: 41tl, 41bl. Consolidated News Pictures Inc/Rex Features: 23t. Corbis: OFCb, 19t, 20-21b, 22, 24t, 28br, 32-33c, 42tr. Federal Bureau of Investigation: 29tr, 43tr, 43b. Fotos International/Rex Features: 4b. Getty Images: 5t, 12t, 15cr, 18bl, 18-19c, 20b, 24-25c, 33t. Stan Honda/AFP/Getty Images: 16-17c. Image from Heroes Comic Book on page 34b: ©2008 Marvel Characters, Inc. Used with permission. iStock: OBCbr, 4t. Doug Kanter/AFP/Getty Images: 16. Pornchai Kittiwongsakul/AFP/Getty Images: 35t. KPA/Zuma/Rex Features: 41br. James Leynse/Corbis: 25t. Brennan Linsley/AFP/Getty Images: 30-31c. Georgi Nadezhdin/AFP/Getty Images: 27b. NBC/Corbis: 9. Bernd Obermann/Corbis: 14t. Erik C Pendzich/Rex Features: 39tr. Rex Features: 6b, 20t, 23b, 28t, 28bl, 30t, 34b, 42tl, 42b. Bob Rowan; Progressive Image/Corbis: 32tl. Ron Sachs/Rex Features: 41tr. Shutterstock: OBCtl, tr, bl, 1, 2, 4-5(background), 6-7(background), 7b, 7t, 8t, 8b, 12b, 13, 17cr, 35b, 36tr, 36b, 37t, 37b, 40l, 48. Sipa Press/Rex Features: 4-5, 17t, 26b, 27t, 29b, 38tl, 39b. STF/AFP/Getty Images: 31t. Charles Sykes/Rex Features: 18t. Mario Tama/Getty Images: OFCtr, OBC background. Time & Life Pictures/Getty Images: 14b. Peter Turnley/Corbis: 15b, 38tr. Universal/Everett/Rex Features: 34t. US Airforce: 40r. Steve Wood/Rex Features: 10.

INTERNATIONAL RUGBY UNION

THE ILLUSTRATED HISTORY

INTERNATIONAL RUGBY UNION

THE ILLUSTRATED HISTORY

PETER BILLS

Foreword by **Sir Clive Woodward**

Featuring exclusive interviews with:

Sir Anthony O'Reilly, Jean-Pierre Lux, Colin Meads, Jean-Pierre Rives, Gareth Edwards, Andrew Slack, Danie Gerber, David Campese, François Pienaar, Martin Johnson & Dan Carter

CARLTON

This book is dedicated to the memory of Lang Jones,
a great man who loved and served the sport of
rugby football all his life. A teacher at King Edward's
School, Bath, for forty years, he was known by
countless numbers in West Country rugby, including
international players and ordinary schoolboys
who played the game under his tutelage. He will
be sorely missed.

Lang Jones 1936–2007

First published as *Rucking & Rolling* in 2007 by
Carlton Books Limited
20 Mortimer Street
London W1T 3JW

This updated edition published in 2011

10 9 8 7 6 5 4 3 2 1

ISBN: 978-1-84732-385-9

Project Art Editor: Luke Griffin
Designer: David Etherington
Picture Research: Paul Langan
Production: Peter Hinton and Janette Burgin
Editorial: Jo Murray
Index: Chris Bell

Printed in Dubai

Several people helped me with this book. I would like to
thank my agent, John Pawsey, who made the connections,
and the design and editorial team at Carlton Books,
who worked with flair and passion to ensure that the book
crossed the try line.

This book does not pretend to be the quintessential record
of the last sixty years of international rugby. What it does
seek to portray are the ebbs and flows of the rugby tide,
a sea that is forever moving and changing.

Previous: The Springboks
team celebrate winning the
William Webb Ellis trophy for
the second time in 2007.

Right: England master kicker
Jonny Wilkinson lands his
fourth and decisive penalty
in the 2007 World Cup
quarter-final against
Australia in Marseille.

Contents

Foreword BY SIR CLIVE WOODWARD

Rugby has experienced sixty years of forward confrontations, of clever, creative running lines by the backs and masterful play by the half-backs, directing their teams to success as surely as a captain his ship to port.

But where to start in highlighting this great sport's major moments in that half century and more? For sure, the game's historical ledger is filled with tales of derring-do, of tries scored, famous match-winning penalties landed and hearts, not to mention the odd limb, broken.

Perhaps we should assess any sport not simply by its score lines – they inevitably fade from the memory – but by the goodwill and friendship it has fostered. And in that respect, rugby union surely attains a prominent position high up on the platform of sports the world has known and revered.

Over sixty years and indeed ever since its creation, this game has offered a helping hand to those in need, a shoulder to lean on for those weary or battered. Great friendships created by the game have flourished into a lifetime's association. Hitherto complete strangers have come to embrace one another, their trust forged completely on the qualities this sport has offered.

Of course, rugby is not alone in that respect but it does have a commendable record. In these pages, you will read not just of Tri-Nations, Triple Crowns or World Cup triumphs. All have their place, but it is people who have been at the core of this game ever since its inception.

The achievements of the great traditional rugby-playing nations of the southern hemisphere, New Zealand and South Africa, are documented, as is Australia's vibrant rise to join its esteemed rivals at the summit of the game south of the Equator. In the northern hemisphere, there is a flavour of the joyous rugby hallmarked by the French and that grand era enjoyed by Wales in the 1970s. England's erratic achievements of earlier years are explored and the tale of their 2003 World Cup success is related. The other Celtic countries, too, have their place, not forgetting the likes of Argentina, Italy and some of the other, hopefully upcoming, nations.

Rugby has known some tumultuous times these past sixty years. The transition to professionalism was, as author Peter Bills writes, delivered as suddenly one morning as a pint of milk on the doorstep. That the sport was woefully under-prepared for that seismic change was always known but that difficult transformation explains some of the continuing problems experienced in the game in countries like England and France.

Days of drama, acts of compassion and magnanimity, events of long-term significance to the entire sport's direction: rugby has known all these times over the course of the last sixty years.

This account, whilst far from pretending to offer the quintessential documentary record of that period, charts the ebbs and flows of the sport through some turbulent waters of that time.

Sir Clive Woodward
2007

Introduction BY PETER BILLS

'Detested sport that owes its pleasures to another's pain,' wrote the English essayist William Cowper in the 18th century.

Well yes, but who wouldn't accept a bit of pain for all the glory, the rip-roaring fun and vibrancy of rugby football?

For sure, the last sixty years of this game in an international sense have been the most fantastic, the most exciting and by far the most dramatic in the entire history of the game. Rugby football in those years has mirrored perfectly 20th-century life: it has opened up, the blinkers have been removed and cast aside.

We've seen dramatic events, great players, fearsome confrontations, acts and deeds that have brought a warm glow to the soul. Like the joyous celebrations of the liberated South African President, Nelson Mandela, upon seeing the Springbok captain François Pienaar lift the 1995 Rugby World Cup for his country in Johannesburg. Has any image in the history of the sport so epitomized what rugby can do, how it can bring people together, provide unity, cohesion and hope where hitherto there were division and doubt?

The last sixty years of rugby football have provided a kaleidoscope of colour, noise and excitement both on and off the playing fields of the world. The coming of the Rugby World Cup signalled the sport's move to a professional code; its old amateur roots were worthy and wondrous, but ultimately untenable in the modern world. To expect young men to give up their time for nothing except the pleasure of the game was a Victorian concept: meritorious and splendid in its day, but with a distinct shelf life. And the irony was, it eventually proved flawed and was undermined by the authorities, those so-called 'guardians' of the amateur ethos, who welcomed into the game sponsors with deep pockets filled with cash. That broke up completely the amateur concept.

This is a sport that has evolved. In the 1950s, as you can read in the pages of this book, fun and frivolity were at the core of the game. Most played it simply as an excuse for the wonderful social life it offered and even those at the highest levels could never be accused of taking it that seriously.

But in some countries of the world, it was a great deal more than a vehicle for laughs. Attitudes in the tough southern hemisphere lands of New Zealand and South Africa were vastly different and those views would ultimately prevail upon the whole world, forcing the countries of the northern hemisphere to adopt a more rigorous approach.

Through the last sixty years, rugby has lured royalty, presidents and prime ministers to its great occasions and, on a more humble level, has been a forum for bringing people together.

All over the world, people associated with this great game continue to do marvellous deeds on its behalf. Young men tragically injured or crippled by accidents on the playing field find friends they never knew existed, as people offer

Opposite: Welsh international full-back Keith Jarrett, who made a stunning international debut against England in Cardiff back in 1967, lines up a goal kick for his club Newport at London Welsh Ground, Old Deer Park, Richmond.

generous financial help or give practical assistance. The term 'rugby's family' is one widely used but it is no mere expression; rather, it is a vibrant, ever eager association offering great bonhomie, kindness and help to anyone requiring it.

On the field these past sixty years, there have been some momentous times. If one had to pick a fantasy team of the world's greatest, perhaps it would be right and proper to focus on the wonderful forwards produced by New Zealand in the 1960s and the great three-quarters who, albeit briefly, put British and Irish rugby on top of the world in the first half of the 1970s.

Becoming an All Black has always been the greatest desire of every living male New Zealander. Typically, they are renowned as strong, powerful forwards with great presence and ball skills. Of course, down the years there have been myriad examples of this particular species but the 1960s seemed to bring together a unique collection of such men. The likes of Wilson Whineray, Colin Meads, Kel Tremain, Brian Lochore, Ken Gray and Waka Nathan were peerless in their class. They helped make New Zealand the greatest rugby nation on earth in their era.

Then, out of the ashes of three losing Lions tours in the 1960s came a squad of British and Irish players who took the world game onto a new, exciting plateau. This was masterminded by a crop of brilliant young Welshmen exuding class and skill: Gareth Edwards, Barry John, Gerald Davies, J. P. R. Williams, Phil Bennett, John Dawes and J. J. Williams. And that was just the backs. When you added on forwards such as Mervyn Davies, John Taylor, Graham Price and his mates in the Pontypool front row it was little wonder that Wales ruled northern hemisphere rugby for most of the 1970s.

And to strengthen the British & Irish Lions for their historic 1971 tour when they became the first (and still the only) Lions touring party in history to win a Test series in New Zealand, there were the likes of Mike Gibson, Ray McLoughlin, Willie John McBride, Fergus Slattery, Gordon Brown, Peter Dixon and David Duckham. Never has the sun shone so brilliantly upon British and Irish rugby.

But who can ignore the talents of so many gifted players in two other major rugby playing lands of the world, South Africa and France? The story of South Africa's evolution over the last fifty years is, for the most part, a painful one. The poisonous apartheid system that, in the end, turned South African against South African had sour repercussions for the sport in the country. Because of it, the Springbok emblem became a pariah in the world game, rejected by all decent and fair-minded people, who were revolted by the political system existing in the country under a dictatorial white regime. It couldn't last and it didn't, but it is still appropriate to enquire of certain international rugby countries and individual players whether, by continuing to send touring parties to that country, they prolonged the agony of apartheid and shored up the blinkered regime in South Africa.

Any activity worthy of its name inevitably strays into the choppy waters of politics and rugby has been no exception. But South Africa's re-emergence as a genuine democratic nation following Mandela's release and the free elections of the early 1990s meant that bitter divisions could be put aside. Most marvellously of all, a new Springbok era dawned, with talented young black players such as Ashwin

Australia's players can only watch as England's fly-half Jonny Wilkinson drops the goal that dramatically wins the 2003 World Cup in Sydney.

Willemse and Bryan Habana earning by right the coveted Springbok jersey. These and so many young men like them have been, and continue to be, outstanding ambassadors not just for their newly unified nation but for the sport in general. Rugby union has been a better game for their presence.

The same can be said of Australia. Given that at the start of the era which this book covers, the 1950s, and for many years thereafter, rugby union in the country was regarded as an also-ran against the omnipresent rugby league, the progress of the sport in that land has been nothing less than sensational. Great men have performed great deeds on behalf of the game in Australia: the likes of Bob Dwyer, Bob Templeton, Alan Jones, the Ella brothers, Andrew Slack, Michael Lynagh, David Campese, John Eales, Michael Foley, Tim Horan and a whole cluster more.

As for the French, so many gloriously talented, unpredictable players have graced the rugby stage. There have been fine, fast ball-handling forwards and wondrous backs blessed with skills and talents honed from youth by the mighty clubs of the country. France has provided the elegance to rugby's staple dish. Without them, the game worldwide would have been so much poorer. But alas, of late, much of that traditional French élan seems to have gone missing, subsumed by a culture of intense coaching that promoted powerful forwards, structure and kicking. France needs to rediscover its flair and old ways to truly flourish.

Meanwhile, other countries such as Argentina, Japan, Italy and the Pacific nations, especially Samoa, continue to have considerable aspirations for the future.

And therein lies the next challenge for the game: the urgent need to offer more opportunities and closer integration to these ambitious countries. It is heartening to see Italy in the Six Nations Championship and Argentina will join the Tri-Nations from 2012, a welcome and long overdue development.

But that is for the future. For the present, let us recall with pleasure the progress of this sport over the last sixty years, reliving briefly through these pages some of the mighty deeds that have captured the imagination of so many in that time.

Peter Bills, 2011

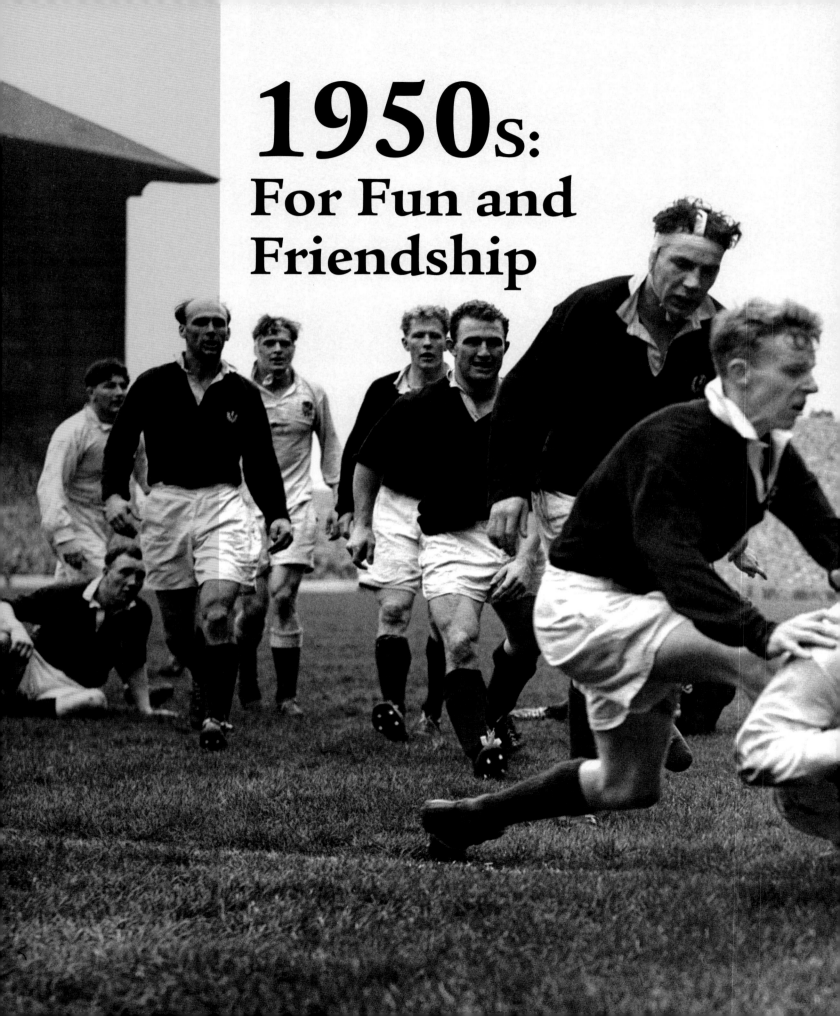

1950s:
For Fun and Friendship

chemist, was working for Glaxo in London and sought out his boss to ask if he might have the following Friday off, 'to go and play for Ireland'.

He was told curtly, 'No, you may not. Go back to your bench. It is not even for England.'

Thompson informed the Irish Rugby Football Union he would not be allowed to meet up the day prior to the match. But strings were pulled, and his release was eventually sanctioned. Yet this spoke volumes about the limited value of even international rugby in the northern hemisphere at that time.

A great dichotomy existed in standards and attitudes between the two hemispheres. Countries of the southern hemisphere like New Zealand and South Africa saw their international rugby team as a worldwide advertisement for their land, one of the driving forces of promotion for the entire country. This was no simple game, something to be taken lightly. The badge of the All Blacks, the famous silver fern, and the dashing, leaping springbok that denoted South Africa, represented statehood.

Australia was by no means the force it was to become, yet here, too, chests swelled with pride when the national jersey was worn. And, as ever with Australians, sport was a highly competitive activity, to be taken seriously. This difference in philosophies was at the root of southern hemisphere hegemony for so many years.

Rugby football of that era was a very different beast to contemporary times. To play with your friends, to tour a faraway country in the southern hemisphere for anything up to six months at a time, was considered the zenith of these young men's ambitions. Sport, just about any sport, still enjoyed the halcyon days of pleasure and pride: certainly in sports that were strictly amateur, the ogre of money was never mentioned. This however, was about to change.

> 'No, you may not. Go back to your bench. It is not even for England.'

Money: The Great Unmentionable

In 1955, the young rugby men of Great Britain and Ireland had been astonished to arrive for the first Test match against South Africa in Johannesburg and witness a vast crowd estimated at as many as 104,000 people. Whatever the precise figure, none of these young rugby tourists had ever seen anything like it. The finances involved for those times were simply staggering, much in excess of anything envisaged in the northern hemisphere.

Then, in 1959, on the British & Irish Lions tour of New Zealand, interest was such that very nearly 800,000 people paid to go and see the tourists, led by Irishman Ronnie Dawson, at their 25 matches on the north and south islands. Remarkably, this represented, at that time, almost half the entire population of that country nestling down in the icy waters, not a thousand miles from the Antarctic wastes.

Opposite: England's Peter Jackson is about to kick to touch against Australia at Twickenham in 1958. England won the close game 9–6.

Wales's Jack Matthews touches down for a try against France in the 1950 Grand Slam win.

Between them, they spent something in the region of £300,000 in tickets to see those Lions, an extraordinary sum of money for those days. Yet the rugby players they had come to see, many of whom had made their reputation four years earlier with the Lions in South Africa, received expenses of just £2 a week: a pittance, an absurdity. Frankly, it represented ridiculous parsimony. Indeed, some had had to put their careers on hold back home, and travelled without any sort of payment whatever from their posts.

The imbalance between around 100,000 people paying good money at the gate to watch players at a single game, in an amateur sport, whilst those players received not a penny for the demonstration of their skills and efforts, not to mention the sacrifices they made in terms of their time and careers, cannot escape the modern-day observer. But in those times, financial gain was never courted, never allowed to stain the name of a game whose very struts were the strict amateur code. Only in France was reality embraced.

But in Britain and Ireland it was considered that those who did wish to pursue money, a vulgar exercise in the eyes of the crusty colonels, madcap majors and those gentlemen who administered rugby union, could join one of the rugby league clubs in the North of England where payment was permitted. Alas, should a player decide to do so, he would render a priest's excommunication something of a slap on the wrist by comparison, so total was the revulsion on the part of those he left behind.

Rugby union accepted with a traditional stiff upper lip the loss of some outstanding talents to the professional code. Lewis Jones, the outstanding Welsh wing, departed in 1952; a few years later, England's fine centre Jeff Butterfield was approached by two men in a wood, whilst out for a training run one day. Introducing themselves without ceremony as the sweating, panting Butterfield looked on bemused, they promptly opened a suitcase they carried with them containing, they assured their target, £6,000 in cash. In those days, that would have been enough for the highly talented, respected English centre to buy a few streets full of houses and a Rolls-Royce. Butterfield smiled and resumed his run.

Nobody could see in those days that there lay at the heart of this great sport, a gross discrepancy, a lie if you like. That lie was buried for decades, the reality ignored, hushed up or rendered irrelevant by the times in which people lived. Thus, the young men making their way into rugby union's dressing rooms and bars of that time, did so for the sheer *joie de vivre*, the fun and love of it all. They carried with them a whiff of the spirit of an earlier generation, young men who had cheerfully sacrificed themselves for the cause of their country. This was different; rugby, after all, was only a game. But the same attitudes prevailed, the same sense of serving the cause, especially at international level. Yet while they played for the fun, the glory and the honour, the unions were quietly making a handsome return from their talents.

England's Jeff Butterfield leads the team out under the watchful eye of the police.

The Lions in South Africa

Those two tours undertaken by the Lions in 1955 and 1959 epitomized the age, the era. Truly, these were rugby union's halcyon days. Arguably, the vintage of 1955 was the best of the two and perhaps the finest Lions ever, matched in class and quality only by the 1971 tourists. They went to a land where men of white Afrikaner background grew huge, their muscles honed by work on the ubiquitous, white-owned farms.

Rugby football was, by a distance, the preferred sporting pastime of these South African people and they revelled in the physicality of the contest.

In 1955, when the Lions selectors sat down to dinner and the task of choosing the thirty players for the tour, they had a delicate assignment. The sensation of the recently concluded Five Nations Championship season was a young Irishman of striking looks, biting humour and intense intellect more befitting a man of many years, than a youngster.

Anthony Joseph Francis O'Reilly possessed a mercurial talent, and he was also immensely gifted as a sportsman. He played rugby, ran the 100 and 200 metres in athletics, excelled at cricket and was a fine tennis player. Yet the man chosen as Lions captain that year, Robin Thompson of Northern Ireland, had warned the selectors prior to their meeting: 'Don't choose O'Reilly; don't spoil him for the future by bringing him on too early. His time will come but this tour is too soon for him. He is too young.'

Thompson was a highly intelligent man but a lousy judge of rugby players. Tony O'Reilly went on the tour, scored twenty tries in twenty-one matches and established a reputation that would be remembered sixty years later. He became, literally, one of rugby's first star players.

O'Reilly impressed everyone with whom he came into contact with his gregarious nature, his confidence, wit and sharp brain. It is the preserve of few young men to enjoy such qualities at 18 years of age. But as the Welsh fly-half of that tour, Cliff Morgan, said memorably, 'At just 18, Tony was the youngest player of all, but he was more like a man of 30, and probably the most intelligent of all.'

The young Irishman possessed a sense of humour every bit as delicious as a fine South African wine. No sooner had those 1955 tourists arrived in the country at Johannesburg airport – the first Lions ever to fly to the southern hemisphere incidentally, albeit via just about every city between London and Johannesburg – than they were taken to watch a provincial match not far from their (then) Transvaal base.

O'Reilly took a look for a short time, mused carefully at what was going on in front of him and turned to a friend and playing colleague beside him. 'Isn't that the biggest, meanest pack of forwards you have ever seen on a rugby field?' he enquired. 'And isn't that ground the hardest you've ever seen in your life to fall on? And isn't there a flight to London from Johannesburg tonight and shouldn't we be on it?'

And so it began, a long, enervating twenty-five-match tour spanning around sixteen weeks. They left London on 16 June and arrived home on the last day of September. They saw sights, sounds and situations beyond the imagination of young men who, in some cases, had hitherto travelled no further than the borders of the British Isles and Ireland.

'South Africa', as someone once noted, 'was renowned both far and wide for politics and little else beside.' The Lions found a whole lot more, however.

Sexual attitudes in countries like Ireland and England in that era, were conventional, to say the least. But what the Lions found when they got to South Africa was a very different scenario. Lions captain Robin Thompson said in 2002 before his death: 'The New Zealand All Blacks had been there in 1949 and afterwards, eight girls whom they had met became pregnant. This was a scandal at the time. But when we got there in 1955, it quickly became clear that you could have slept with a married or single woman every night of the tour, if you'd wanted to. The women just threw themselves at you everywhere you went. The girls were from really well-to-do families. Some of them travelled all around the country, just following the Lions. They were educated, monied women; it was astonishing. Today, they would be called groupies.

'It was a real eye-opener at that time because remember, we had come from Britain and Ireland in the mid-1950s when getting your hands on a girl's breasts was an achievement. So it shocked everybody in the party how amoral sexually South Africa was. It was one of the most amazing things at that time bearing in mind the innate conservatism of the country. But we quickly came to realize it was a false conservatism. Most of the women out there had servants and nothing else to do.'

In fact, the ultra-conservative Lions management was so concerned that when they heard one player was involved with a woman, the manager is alleged to have threatened to write to the player's parish priest.

As for the rugby, a dramatic first Test at Johannesburg's famous Ellis Park lured around 100,000 South Africans to witness what came to be known as one of the most famous games in the long history of the sport. It was decided in the Lions favour, 23 points to 22, only because the South African full-back Jack van der Schyff missed a last-minute conversion that would have won the game.

South Africans took the sport deadly seriously; this was no pastime for fun, friendship and relaxation. In their eyes South Africa was the most powerful rugby nation on earth, had never (at that time) lost a Test series to the feared New Zealanders and an opening Test defeat by the Lions went down as badly as a tumbling gold price on the high veld. The South African prime minister went into the Lions dressing room after the game to announce: 'Well done, but this is a terrible day for South Africa'. The Lions players thought he was joking; alas,

> 'Isn't that the biggest, meanest pack of forwards you have ever seen on a rugby field? And isn't that ground the hardest you've ever seen in your life to fall on? And isn't there a flight to London ... And shouldn't we be on it?'

Following pages: British & Irish Lion Billy Williams is pursued by the Springbok forward Salty Du Rand as he kicks the ball up-field. South Africa won this fourth Test played at Port Elizabeth 22–8.

he was deadly serious. The next day, one of the local newspapers had a cartoon drawing of the Prime Minister and the South African rugby selectors walking up the plank onto a ship named *Abroad*. It was taken that seriously.

This was the contrast between attitudes in the northern and southern hemispheres. The Springboks played to win; nothing else mattered. Their supporters demanded victory as an extension of their imagined supremacy as a people. Losing to anyone could not be tolerated.

Thus, whilst the Lions played schoolboy jokes on each other, furtively (in the case of the late Clem Thomas) collected, stored and then sold for profit the packets of cigarettes handed to players as gifts, and enjoyed themselves in the most self-indulgent of activities, the South Africans were addressing the ramifications of that first Test defeat as though it were an early battle in a war. For them it was.

They trained assiduously, prepared extensively and adopted an approach that was akin to professionalism. It paid off in the form of a 25-9 victory in the second Test at Cape Town, but was again found wanting as the Lions took a tightly contested third Test, 9-6, at Pretoria, a city at the very heart of Afrikanerdom. The locals were beside themselves with despair and anger.

> 'It quickly became clear that you could have slept with a married or single woman every night of the tour, if you'd wanted to.'

Take the message the 1955 South African team captain, Stephen Fry, received from one irate supporter following the Springboks' third Test defeat at Pretoria. 'Dear Mr Fry,' it read, 'It is high time that you opened your eyes and realized that as far as football is concerned, you are a failure. The sooner you say farewell to the game and withdraw entirely from the team, the better it will be for your health.

'If you ignore this warning it will be too late for sorrow. You have very likely received several similar letters. The only difference between those and this one is that if you ignore it you will not have the pleasure of leaving the field as Stephen Fry. Indeed, the title "late" will appear before your name. Even if I have to pay for it with my own life I will do so willingly, for I will know that I have done so in the interests of our national game.'

By wonderful contrast with all this intensity, a couple of the Lions players devised cunning ploys to find the best parties in town on their tour and get themselves invited on a Saturday evening after the match. 'We used to drive up to Jan Smuts Avenue, one of the smartest areas of Johannesburg, in a car someone had lent us for the evening,' recalled Irish three-quarter Cecil Pedlow. 'We'd see a lot of cars parked outside a house, see all the lights on and knock on the door.

'We'd say something like, "Oh, do you know where so and so road is", or "do you know where the Van Rensburgs live?" Of course, they were all hypothetical. But we'd be wearing our Lions blazers and ties and suddenly, there'd be a shout from the guy at the front door – "Hey, it's Tony O'Reilly and his pal from the Lions at the door."

'Of course, we'd be invited in, entertained regally and have a wonderful time. It always worked.'

The scowling, snarling, sweating Springboks were enduring a rather less riotous preparation for their last meeting with the tourists. They simply had to triumph in the final Test at Port Elizabeth and against a tired, injury-ravaged and, in some cases, homesick Lions team, they did, 22-8. It tied the series at 2-2 but few could escape the conclusion that the Lions had, over the course of their twenty-five games (nineteen of which were won) provided rugby of a supreme quality and attraction. The darting, fleet-footed backs, players like O'Reilly, Morgan and the English centre Jeff Butterfield, one of the finest passers of a ball the game had known, had exposed many leaden-footed opponents. These Lions had possessed not just quality but class, on and off the field.

And they had fun. As Cliff Morgan said some time later, 'It was an adventure. It wasn't all about winning matches, about tactics, about watching endless videotapes. It was fun.'

Bryn Meredith and Rees Williams of the Lions rush to block a kick from the Springbok scrum-half Tommy Gentles during the first Test at Ellis Park, Johannesburg in 1955. The Lions won 23-22.

The International Rugby Grounds

International grounds of yesteryear were rudimentary affairs. Splinters in the backside and aching muscles were all part of the day out, and that was for the so-called lucky ones who had seats.

Few of the old grounds had many comforts. They were unrecognizable to the swank, modern stadiums of contemporary times.

Cardiff Arms Park was another place of strictly limited facilities, for players and spectators. Those attending matches readied themselves to be crammed in on international match days, but as for the atmosphere; well, it was raw-boned and unique. They poured out of the city pubs just across the street from the stadium to roar their support for their beloved Wales. Curiously, the old ground doubled up as a greyhound track and those familiar lights that lit up the racing dogs provided an odd backdrop for international rugby games.

Murrayfield, where Scotland played, had vast banks of terracing and an unknown capacity. It is said that for one match against Wales in the 1960s, around 110,000 people squeezed in, thousands of them sitting on the touchline or behind the dead-ball line at each end.

Twickenham, full of those little wooden, splinter-filled seats just waiting to jag into the unwary bottom, was smaller but more intimate. Those sitting just inside the little wooden fence that ran around the ground had a wonderful insight into the game, able to hear players' calls and comments.

If, in later years, you wanted to know what these old stadiums were like, you could have visited Ireland's Lansdowne Road until the end of 2006 (when demolition and rebuilding was due to begin). There, you could see the basic accommodation, the comparative lack of hospitality space (although the west stand on the ground did contain some boxes for corporate entertainment).

In countries of the southern hemisphere, vast stands of tubular steel were erected, stretching high into the sky. Ellis Park had a towering stand that looked perilous but it offered a bird's-eye view of the game below. Great crowds of close to 100,000 could be accommodated.

Newlands Stadium, Cape Town, was built beneath the imposing Table Mountain range that dominates the Cape. Its stands were never quite as high as some built at Ellis Park, nor as perilous-looking. But if the rugby was not special to watch on a particular day, spectators could enjoy the wonderful views of the mountains at the back of the ground.

In Wellington, New Zealand, another huge stand was erected on the Athletic Park site at the southern end of the city. Those who sat in the top half of it, which was all open to the elements, would invariably be wind-lashed and feel the driving rain from one of those familiar southerly gales that batter the rugged coastline in winter.

Opposite: The old Cardiff Arms Park with the famous greyhound track around the perimeter.

Left: Twickenham Stadium is affectionately known as the 'Cabbage Patch' on account that the land where the ground stands was previously used to grow the vegetable.

Below: The original Murrayfield Stadium opened in 1925. The first visitors were England, whom Scotland beat to win their first Five Nations Championship Grand Slam.

Above: Newlands Stadium, Cape Town as it looked in the 1950s. The first international was held in 1891 when the British and Irish Lions toured South Africa.

Left: French internationals at the Colombes Stadium, Paris were renowned for being noisy, exuberant affairs. The ground was originally constructed for the 1924 Olympic Games.

crossing the Severn Bridge in a westerly direction and finding themselves at places like Swansea, Cardiff, Newport, Llanelli, Pontypool, Abertillery or Neath knew what to expect. That tough preparation each week readied the top Welsh players for international rugby, whereas England's players might have a couple of relatively competitive games a month interspersed by two absurdly one-sided encounters. Amazingly, this was a problem England would struggle to come to terms with for another thirty years. Indeed, it wasn't really until the late 1980s when leagues were at last introduced into the English club scene, that things began to change.

Then there were the farcical selections and overt favouritism of the England selectors. In 1955, Englishman Dickie Jeeps had been considered good enough to become first choice scrum-half in all four Test matches for the British and Irish Lions. Not only that, he excelled with Cliff Morgan as his half-back partner and impressed everyone with his courage, doughty abilities and service.

Alas, the England selectors knew better. Jeeps, uncapped prior to that tour, played only one Test of the 1956 Five Nations Championship and it wasn't until the following year that he won another cap.

England were Five Nations Champions in 1953, Triple Crown winners (and Championship runners-up) in 1954, runners-up again in 1956, Champions and Grand Slam winners in 1957 and Champions again in 1958. As with Wales, they had built their sustained meritocracy on the backs of some outstandingly talented players, the likes of centres Jeff Butterfield and W. P. C. Davies, wings Peter Jackson and Peter Thompson, scrum-half Jeeps plus forwards like Eric Evans, Ron Jacobs, David Marques and John Currie at lock forward and fine back-row players like Alan Ashcroft, Reg Higgins and 'Tug' Wilson.

> 'For Christ's sake, Pete – I'm on duty and I'm trying to follow someone.'

In 1955 against France at Twickenham, England included Wilson, a London police officer, and Peter Yarranton, the Wasps forward, in their side. The build-up to the game in the early part of the week contained an unusual incident.

Yarranton was strolling down a London street on the Tuesday evening, with some friends, after a few beers in a local hostelry. The boys were in fine fettle: Yarranton was playing against France on Saturday, the beer had been good and all seemed right with the world. Although it was dark, Yarranton cast his gaze across the street and, lo and behold, who was there in the shadows but Tug Wilson, with whom he would play for his country four days later in the international.

'I started waving and shouting across the street to Tug, but found it most odd – he completely ignored me,' Yarranton told me, years later. 'So, like all good Englishmen who cannot make themselves heard, I shouted louder: "Tug, Tug; how are you".' At which point Wilson came scuttling across the street, rushed up to Yarranton and said, 'For Christ's sake, Pete, shut up – I'm on duty and I'm trying to follow someone!'

Someone who was to become rather well known in British political life in later years, Denis Thatcher, husband of Conservative Prime Minister Margaret Thatcher, was one of the touch judges for the 1956 Five Nations Championship match in the Championship, retired after a distinguished career of 33 caps spanning eight seasons. Then came the great Jean Prat who won a remarkable 51 caps from 1945 to 1955, an extraordinary total for those days.

Prat was a legend in his playing days and, in retirement, became revered throughout the land as a colossus of the sport. When he died, in his beloved Lourdes, in 2005, almost the entire town not to mention rugby men from all over France, turned out for his funeral. He had given French rugby great presence.

When he had retired, the role of 'Le Général' passed to the great Lucien Mias and it fell to that fine forward from the Mazamet club to lead France to their first ever Five Nations Championship title in 1959.

They'd been trying, on and off, since 1910 and even though they lost to Ireland and drew with England, victories over Scotland and Wales were enough to give them their triumph.

Nowadays, French club rugby is dominated by a small handful of clubs, most notably Biarritz, Toulouse and Stade Français. On the next level down you find the likes of Perpignan, Agen, Bourgoin and Clermont Auvergne. But take a look at some of the clubs whose players made up France's 1954 winning team against Scotland: FC Lourdes, Racing Club de France, CS Bourg, US Bressane, US Cognac, Aviron Bayonnais, Tarbes and Vienne. Many of them have now virtually disappeared, or are no longer anywhere near the top flight.

Yet Lourdes was once pre-eminent as the most powerful club in France, certainly of the 1950s. They won the coveted French Championship title, the 'Bouclier de Brennu', in 1952, 1953, 1956, 1957, 1958 and 1960, as well as being runners-up in 1955. Lourdes had the great players of the age, like the wonderfully talented Prat brothers, Jean and Maurice, Jean Barthe, Roger Martine, Henri Domec, André Labazuy, Pierre Lacaze and others. These were players of consummate skills and talent, men who had learned the essential basics of the game as youngsters in their local French communities and moved seamlessly into top-class rugby. They brought a great style, a panache to the game in France and indeed, wherever they played.

Whatever their proclivities off the field, the French added immensely to the colour and gaiety of the old Championship. When they were in the mood, they played rugby to make the gods smile, the ball flashing down a three-quarter line where *vitesse, vitesse, plus de vitesse* was the critical factor. None of the French wings had greater gas than Alain Porthault of the suitably named Racing Club de France, who played international rugby for three seasons from 1951 to 1953. Porthault was so fast he was a semi-finalist in the 100m at the Youth Olympics in Helsinki.

Teams visiting Paris generally had the time of their lives on a Saturday evening at the after-match banquet. Indeed, the Irish pair Tony O'Reilly and Andy Mulligan decided after a match there one year that the girls looked so pretty, the spring sunshine was so warm and beguiling and the hospitality so omnipresent that they should stay on for a few days, which they promptly did. These are pleasures denied to the later generations of players.

The official programme for the 1959 match between Blackheath and a star-studded Barbarians team.

Opposite: France captain Jean Prat, nicknamed 'Mr Rugby' by the English press after the first French win at Twickenham in 1951. The flanker, who could kick exceptionally well, won 51 caps, 17 as captain, between 1945 and 1955.

Sir Anthony O'Reilly

Ireland 1955–70

Centre and Wing

Tony O'Reilly won 29 caps for Ireland between 1955 and 1970, mainly as a centre, but it was as a wing for the British & Irish Lions, first in South Africa in 1955 and in New Zealand four years later, that he played his greatest rugby. By a long distance, he remains the Lions' leading try scorer, and scored six in his ten Tests as a Lion.

'In 1959 we could easily have won the Test series 3-1. But in the first Test we had a referee who gave an appalling performance. He was basically incompetent, but we have to remember he was the home referee in that region. So we lost to six penalty goals despite scoring four tries. Yet on modern-day scoring we would have won 25-18, a point of which I always remind Sir Wilson Whineray, one of our opponents that day, when I see him!

Those were times of fun and friendship. But also ferocity, too, occasionally. We had some marvellous players in that era; that was what made it special. On the 1955 tour there was the magic of Cliff Morgan, which can never be forgotten. He was probably the best fly-half ever to leave these shores, with Jack Kyle (who toured New Zealand in 1950) his co-equal. On the hard grounds of Africa, Morgan was fantastic.

We had such fun on that tour and we just ran and ran for five months; that's what I remember. We also used the little kick over the top of the defence or the grubber kick through to make our opponents turn and defend. I wonder why players don't use those tactics far more to defeat the rush defence in the modern-day game for there is much room to be exploited behind that on-rushing defence.

We were the first Lions team to tour there since 1938 and the interest was enormous. But the hard grounds certainly suited our style of play.

New Zealand in 1959 was very different. It was often rainy and the wet and the mud slowed our game down. We were introduced to a style of New Zealand play very much more concentrated on forwards than anything we had seen in South Africa or Australia. Colin Meads typified that.

Opposite: A young Tony O'Reilly lines up before one of his early games for Ireland.

I remember the New Zealand Rugby Union President Gordon Brown attempting to defend their win with all those penalties at a tumultuous dinner in Dunedin after the first Test. It was one of the worst nights for New Zealand rugby; we should have won and most New Zealanders were ashamed to see their team win. But Brown said at the dinner they had won "within the framework of the rules" and that became a catchphrase (and excuse) for any sort of jocularity on the remainder of our tour. Even if questioned by our officials for a few incidents, we would repeat the mantra, "But we did it within the framework of the rules". It produced no end of fun.

I would say the most gifted Lions teams I have seen would be our 1955 side in South Africa and the 1971 team in New Zealand. The 1959 Lions would be close to them and, of course, the 1974 Lions were undefeated in South Africa, which was a fine achievement. Perhaps they lacked the skill and verve in the back line. But those sides would have to be the best of that century. In 1971 and 1974 you have to say there was a bit more attrition than in my day, perhaps warfare in 1974 in South Africa.

So although I would doff my hat to certain members of the 1950 Lions such as Jack Kyle, Lewis Jones, Bleddyn Williams and Jack Matthews, I believe the 1955 and 1971 Lions were the best. Barry John and Gareth Edwards were a remarkable pair of half-backs on the 1971 tour but I wouldn't put them ahead of our 1955 halves, Dickie Jeeps and Cliff Morgan.

The great thing about the current Irish squad is that they actually have about twenty players of real international calibre. Strength in depth is crucial, absolutely critical in the modern game, and this Irish squad is terrific in that respect. I am lost in admiration for their overall quality and strength.

Ronan O'Gara's kicking is brilliant, quite exceptional. Then you have the incredible work rate of Brian O'Driscoll. What is so wonderful about him is that his attacking play is so exceptionally good yet even without the ball, O'Driscoll is a heroic defender.

As for the forwards, Ireland has the outstanding Paul O'Connell in the second row. He is, arguably, the finest all-round lock in world rugby. He represents all the virtues of Irish forward play. He is one of the best Irish locks I have ever seen. Robin Thompson, who captained the 1955 Lions, Willie John McBride and Moss Keane were all fine locks, but O'Connell is terrific.

Opposite: Tony O'Reilly on a typically determined run for the British & Irish Lions.

1960s:
The Slumbering of a Giant

By contrast, Scotland and Ireland did a little better. The Scots began the decade by losing twice to South Africa, 18-10 in Port Elizabeth in 1960 and 12-5 in Edinburgh the following year. But in 1964, they achieved what no other side managed: they held the touring All Blacks to a 0-0 draw at Murrayfield. The next year they beat South Africa at Murrayfield 8-5 and followed that with a 1966 win over Australia at Murrayfield by 11 points to 5, a distinguished trinity of triumphs. True, New Zealand beat them in Edinburgh on their next tour, 1967, by 14 points to 3, but in 1968 Scotland again toppled the Wallabies, 9-3 in Edinburgh. Finally, in 1969, they again beat the Springboks at Murrayfield, 6-3.

These were encouraging results in the context of the virtual wasteland that was being experienced by the players of England and Wales against southern hemisphere opponents. What is more, Ireland also had some good results.

They had beaten a southern hemisphere nation for the first time in 1958, Australia in Dublin, and although they lost to South Africa in 1960 in Dublin (3-8) and in 1961 in Cape Town (24-8), as well as being narrowly defeated 6-5 by the All Blacks in Dublin in 1963, better things were around the corner.

They beat South Africa 9-6 in Dublin in 1965, then had a hat-trick of wins against the Australians. They won 15-8 in Dublin in 1967, 11-5 in Sydney a few months later and then 10-3 at Lansdowne Road the following year.

What most of these results underlined was the gap that continued to exist between the southern hemisphere major rugby-playing nations and the countries of the northern hemisphere. True, the playing field was slightly evened up when the southern hemisphere countries embarked on their (then) long tours of the UK, Ireland and France. But there was an intensity, a dedication and an importance known to all rugby men in countries like New Zealand and South Africa that simply wasn't the same elsewhere.

The Australians were battling hard to exist so close to the powerful Kiwis, and they unearthed some players of supreme skills in that era, such as half-backs Ken Catchpole and Phil Hawthorne plus Tony Miller, in the pack.

What Vivien Jenkins described as 'competition taken to the extreme' was typified by a trio of incidents involving the legendary New Zealand lock forward Colin Meads in the later years of the 1960s.

In December 1967, playing for New Zealand against Scotland at Murrayfield, Meads was warned in the first half by the Irish referee Kevin Kelleher for dangerous play. But later in the game the All Black appeared to launch a kick that caught Scottish fly-half David Chisholm and was sent off. It was the first dismissal of an All Black since Cyril Brownlee in 1924. Meads was suspended for two tour games but the ignominy was far greater than the short period of absence from the game.

Some New Zealand commentators called it an injustice yet just six months later, in June 1968 whilst playing for the All Blacks against Australia in the first Test at the Sydney Cricket Ground, the brilliant Wallaby scrum-half Ken Catchpole found himself trapped awkwardly in a ruck. Meads unaware of Catchpole's inability to move, grabbed his leg and wrenched it in an effort to

Opposite: 'Mine!'
Powerful New Zealand lock
Colin Meads grabs the ball,
a familiar sight in the 1960s.

The official programme for Gareth Edwards' debut match for Wales against the French in Paris. France won 20-14.

move him off the ball. He literally tore almost all the player's groin muscles to shreds. The screams of agony could be heard in several parts of the ground.

Catchpole had made his international debut in 1961 and by this time was regarded as one of the greatest scrum-halves in the world. He had won 27 caps. Alas, the damage inflicted by Meads's action meant that he never played again. It was a sad, brutal end to a fine international career.

The following year, in May 1969, in the Christchurch Test match between New Zealand and Wales, Meads punched the Welsh hooker Jeff Young so hard that the player's jaw was fractured and he took no further part in the tour.

But Meads knew how to take blows and suffer pain himself. In August 1970, he played a Test match against South Africa in Port Elizabeth with only a protective cast covering his broken arm.

Colin Meads played fifty-five Tests for New Zealand in a career of great longevity spanning the years 1957–71. Today, he is, perhaps only after Sir Wilson Whineray, regarded as the greatest living All Black. But the excesses by which he risked staining his reputation were regarded as justifiable by most New Zealanders. South Africans of that era would also have subscribed to such a viewpoint.

But it was in stark contrast to the opinions existing at the time in the countries of the British Isles and Ireland. Of course, the French could mix it, and often did. Violence frequently marred their matches, with fistfights a feature of games, especially at club level. When local pride was at stake no Frenchman worthy of the name would take a step back. As someone once wrote 'If you want to interest a Frenchman in a game, you tell him it's a war. But if you want to interest an Englishman in a war you tell him it's a game.'

At international level, the French did what they do best: unpredictability. In 1961, on their New Zealand tour, they lost all three Tests, 13-6, 5-3 and a thumping 32-3. Three years later when the countries met again, they lost 12-3 in Paris, and in 1967 on the same Stade Colombes ground, once more went down, 21-15.

Things were more encouraging against the Springboks. The two countries drew 0-0 in Paris in 1961 before France won 8-6 at Springs, on the Eastern Transvaal, in 1964. In 1967, France undertook a four-Test-match tour of South Africa. They lost the first two games, 26-3 in Durban and 16-3 in Bloemfontein. Yet from the ashes of such defeats the French put together a performance good enough to snatch a 19-14 Test win in Johannesburg. The series was still alive as they went to Cape Town for the decider.

Both sides could have won it, but a 6-6 draw meant the Springboks just edged the series. A year later, there was more South African success with Test wins in Bordeaux (12-9) and in Paris, by 16 points to 11.

Matches with Australia provided some solace for France, with Test match victories in 1961 in Sydney, 15–8 points and in Paris in 1967 by 20 points to 14. Australia won 11-10 when the two sides met again in Sydney in 1968.

Interestingly, the emerging Romanians gave France more trouble than Australia in the 1960s, beating them in 1960, 1962 and 1968 and drawing in 1961 and 1963.

Opposite: The colossal French captain Walter Spanghero leading his team out.

The Five Nations Championship

If the 1950s had been Wales's era in the old Five Nations Championship, then it would have been the same in the 1960s, but for one country: France. Between them, the two nations dominated the Championship throughout this decade, winning the title in nine of the ten years. Only England, in 1963, briefly managed to break the monopoly.

As before, substitutions remained a far-off dream. At Murrayfield in January 1960, French wing Lucien Roge broke his hand but had to play on, because no replacements were allowed under the law. France just edged home despite the handicap, 13-11, and in winning three of their four games with the other drawn, took the title.

They retained it the following year, 1961, for the third season in succession, building their success once more around the quality and experience of players like Michel Celaya, François Moncla and Michel Vannier, all of whom featured in

France's Guy Camberabero converts the first French try in a match against England at Twickenham in 1967. France won 16-12 and Camberabero finished the championship with a then record points total of 32.

France's three successive Championship titles. At the end of this season, all three would end their international careers, but France had new men of class and talent waiting to step into their shoes.

For all of the Five Nations competitors it was a time for introducing new caps. In 1960 at Twickenham, England beat Wales 14-6 with a side that contained six backs holding just 14 caps between them. Two years later, Ireland went to Twickenham with an astonishing 9 new caps. They'd been pulling them onto the bus as they drove along the motorway the Irish were building to Twickenham, someone joked. Predictably, Ireland lost 16-0 that day, yet two of the new men, Ray McLoughlin and Willie John McBride, were to become among Ireland's greatest ever forwards. Then, in 1965, the entire cap total for the England side that lost to Ireland in Dublin was just 69 and two years later, England took 8 new caps to Ireland and won, 8-3.

'Out with the old, in with the new,' seemed to be a catchphrase that epitomized the selectors' views at this time.

And Five Nations seasons in those days, in an era of fixture lists uncluttered by too many competitions, just went on and on. The 1960 Championship began on 9 January and did not finish until 9 April, an extraordinary span of over twelve weeks.

1962 saw France retain their title and dominance, a consistency matched only by Ireland's completely contrasting fortunes. Bottom in 1960, 1961 and 1962, they finished second from bottom in 1963 and then bottom again in 1964. It was as well that the Irish retained their sense of humour, on and off the field. Like the front-row forward who went up to his captain during a break in play and angrily thrust his forearm in front of the leader's gaze.

'Look at my arm' he exclaimed, mumbling and spluttering with fury. 'That bastard over there's bitten me.' And sure enough, there were the teeth marks.

His captain looked puzzled.

'Why are you mumbling? And why don't you go and bite him back?', asked the skipper.

'I'd like to,' he replied, 'only, I can't. I've left my false teeth in the changing room.'

And then there was the wizard jape pulled by one London Irish player, Kevin Lavelle, a Royal Navy sailor who found himself marooned one day on the *Ark Royal* in the Bay of Naples. Lavelle was summoned to his captain's cabin and addressed as follows: 'Well now, Lavelle, we have had a request to release you to play rugby for Ireland. Now normally we don't allow this sort of thing, but in the circumstances, we are prepared to do so. Have your bags ready at 0900.'

Lavelle did as he was told. With a smirk on his face.

At 0900, a helicopter landed on deck and whisked him to the nearest air base from where he was flown to London. He went straight to Sunbury-on-Thames, home of London Irish, was royally received and played the club match the following afternoon. A long evening of riotous celebration followed.

Alas, as with all such escapades, there was a price to pay. When the Navy heard the truth, Lavelle was for the high jump. 'I was in irons for a month after they found out,' he told a pal.

'But,' he added, in the spirit of those times, 'it was worth it.'

Watching the French at that time was invariably worth it. If something dazzling and spectacular wasn't happening on the field, it was off it, in the selectors' room. A defeat would bring forth the guillotine and a new bunch thrust into the fray. French selectors played fast and loose with players' careers throughout that era. Yet increasingly, they had the players to try, and a new batch always seemed ready to step up.

As a year, 1963 was an aberration in terms of the total dominance of France and Wales in that decade. It was a suitably bizarre, topsy-turvy Championship. Scotland won in Paris, England in Cardiff, France in Dublin, Wales in Edinburgh and Ireland in Cardiff. At Twickenham in the second half of March, England's attacking fly half

> 'Why are you mumbling? And why don't you go and bite him back?'

'Imagine then my thoughts when I was chosen for only my second cap to play against them at the start of that 1960 series. To go on the field against them was awesome. For at least six months before they arrived, the build-up, expectation and excitement was immense. You just wanted to play at that high level.

'The scores give an indication of how close the series was and it was the first time that I understood what international rugby meant. We won the first Test 13-0 but lost the second, 11-3. The third Test at Bloemfontein was drawn 11-all after the All Blacks scored 8 points in the last five minutes. So the series was decided in the last Test, at Port Elizabeth, and it was a hard battle which we just edged 8-3.

'I remember walking with the team to the cinema one evening before one of those Test matches. As we were leaving the hotel, we walked past the New Zealanders who were going somewhere else. Things were so tense, we didn't even greet one another. Not a man on either side raised a 'Hello, how is it going?' or anything like that. You kept your head down and kept walking until you were past them.

'In fact, in 1964 for the South African jubilee when several overseas players were invited to attend, we got to know some of the New Zealanders quite well. So we knew them better when we went to New Zealand for the 1965 series, under the captaincy of Dawie de Villiers. Unfortunately, we lost that series 3-1 and New Zealand's 20-3 win in the final Test at Auckland was their biggest ever over us at that time. They scored five tries to none that day.

'Playing New Zealand was something else, it was so physically hard. You knew you'd had a game of rugby, all right.'

'I would say those four Tests in 1960 were the hardest, the toughest, the most pressurized Test matches I ever played in. It was the most intense rugby you could imagine. When we went to the UK and played all the international teams over there later that year, it was nowhere near as intense. The northern hemisphere teams weren't at the same level; playing New Zealand was something else, it was so physically hard. You knew you'd had a game of rugby, all right. You needed two to three days to get your body together after one of those Tests. It was that hard and tough.

'One match we played on our 1960/61 tour to Britain and Ireland, on the English south coast, left me with an extraordinary memory of rugby in the Britain at that time. We'd been staying at Eastbourne and when we got to the ground, we saw our opponents' coach pull up and they were singing. We were ready to chew leather, bite stones as we'd been used to in the highly physical contests against the All Blacks. But here were our English opponents singing songs in the build-up to a game. We couldn't believe that.

'But the British and Irish sides only used to get together on a Friday and toss the ball around among themselves. Yet they had some great players who could play, as was proven by the fact that we only beat England 5-0, Scotland 12-5, Ireland 8-3 and Wales 3-0, whilst we drew 0-0 with France in Paris. It rather proved that the UK, Irish and French teams did have good players.'

Previous pages: New Zealand scrum-half Kevin Bricoe prepares to off-load possession against the Springboks in 1960.

Opposite: One of the best. New Zealand's Kel Tremain a superb player, kicks as Welsh wing Dewi Bebb tackles.

Jean-Pierre Lux

France 1967–75

Wing and Centre

Jean-Pierre Lux made his international rugby debut for France in 1967 and won 47 caps before his retirement in 1975. He carved a reputation as a quick, clever, elusive back. Today, he is Chairman of the ERC, the body that runs the highly successful Heineken Cup competition in European rugby.

'I have two favourite memories from that time. One was my first game for France, for to beat England at Twickenham was very special. Guy Camberabero also played his first game for France in that match. When you are young, only 20 years old, you are on the field and during the game you just play and think of the rugby. It is only before the game and after, that you look at the stadium, you see the people.

1968 was an extraordinary season because halfway through the Championship, we had a game between a French XV and a South-East XV in Grenoble. It was a very bad game for France and after that the selectors changed half the team. But at that time we had many good players, so the selectors could make many changes. We could have had two very good teams. Yet it was still a time when rugby was not that serious in attitude. I was a student and I had my work, so I trained only one or two times a week. I could not spend much time training.

You would say my studies were more important to me then than my rugby although I was pleased and proud to be chosen for France. The southern hemisphere nations were more powerful and we were reminded of that both in 1967 when we played in South Africa and after our Grand Slam in 1968. We went to New Zealand on tour that summer and it was very difficult to play the All Blacks.

When we arrived in South Africa we saw the power of the South African players and it was a wonderful sight, something we had not seen before. They had bigger, more powerful physical players than any country in the northern hemisphere. That was the biggest difference at that time. I played centre and the South African centres were very, very strong. When I ran out and saw the size of them, I thought

Opposite: Lux in full flight against Wales. He was renowned for his excellent ball handling and acute awareness.

Jean-Pierre **LUX**

to myself, "This is going to be most difficult". We saw the South African team training before the first Test and we thought "Oh, là là!"

But after we lost the first two Tests, we won the third and drew the last so it was a good tour. It was much the same the year after in New Zealand where we lost the three Test matches, although we won in Australia. Those were very hard tours physically. It is never easy to beat New Zealand but it was even harder then because attitudes were different.

In 1970, England came to Stade Colombes in the Championship and we had a wonderful match against them. It was champagne rugby and we won 35-13. I scored one of our six tries that day. Two years later at Colombes, we won 37-12. Again, we scored six tries and I got one of them. That remains a special memory for me, not least because it was the last game France ever played at Colombes.

Recently, I saw a film of that match and it was an extraordinary game, full of running, attacking rugby. Of course, it was a pleasure to play in if you were French. England had some good players, like David Duckham and John Spencer, but they were not a good team.

Of course, there has been a rugby revolution since those times. Therefore, it is not possible to play like that any more because defences are so much tighter now and the physical potential of players is so much better. I still think sides have to try and attack even in today's rugby, but some clubs do not try to play or pass the ball. For me, that is a shame.

It was not really until the 1970s that rugby started to become much more serious in the northern hemisphere. In the Sixties, you still had fun most of the time. But the increasing influence of television and the growing numbers of people who watched the Five Nations Championship matches helped to change attitudes and make people take the game more seriously. It forced changes in preparation, too.

In the 1970s, France changed its style under Jacques Fouroux. Suddenly, you had big forwards dominating the play and it wasn't the same. French rugby changed greatly from the 1960s to the 1970s but the style of the 1970s was a rugby that meant we could win consistently, and winning became more important. Before that, you wanted to win of course but having fun and pleasure was the most important thing.

Opposite: Jean-Pierre Lux touching down against England at Colombes in 1970. France demolished their opponents, winning 35-13.

Colin Meads
New Zealand 1957–71
Lock

Colin Meads made his debut for the All Blacks in 1957 and went on to win 55 caps. Meads was an industrious, fiercely committed lock forward who forged a reputation as one of the toughest forwards ever to play the game.

'New Zealand and South Africa were the strongest teams in the game. But what also made those series so special was that we only used to meet the Springboks every five to six years; that was all.

The great aura of the Springboks meeting the All Blacks that existed in our day has now gone and the reason is they play each other every year these days. That has reduced the importance of it.

I have to say, not being able to win a Test series in South Africa represents one of the real low points of my career. We were right in it in 1960 and 1970 but the fact that we didn't quite do it meant that subsequently we always felt that as a team we had let ourselves down. By contrast, beating South Africa in New Zealand in 1965 was a high but you felt they were always one-up on us and that was a national calamity.

It was very hard to win over there, especially with local referees. There was always this perceived bias and it affected all teams who toured in the southern hemisphere. The only time we had neutral referees was when we went to the northern hemisphere and a Welshman, for example, would referee the England–New Zealand Test match.

But it wasn't just tough playing South Africa – it was hard enough when we went on tour to the northern hemisphere. We would leave in September and play right through to February and by then, the northern hemisphere countries were getting right up for it. They never did the intense training prior to the start of their season – they seemed to play to get fit. But after Christmas they were definitely getting there, which probably explains results like our 0-0 draw with Scotland in Edinburgh in early 1964. And we had a bit of trouble in Ireland on that tour, I seem to recall. They ran us very close, 6-5. As for Wales, they were always one of our biggest enemies on the field. England weren't as strong then as they eventually became in later years.

With the Lions it was different. We sat and waited for them; it was always a big

Opposite: A hugely committed player, Colin Meads became only the second player in union history to be sent off in an international against Scotland at Murrayfield in 1967.

Colin MEADS

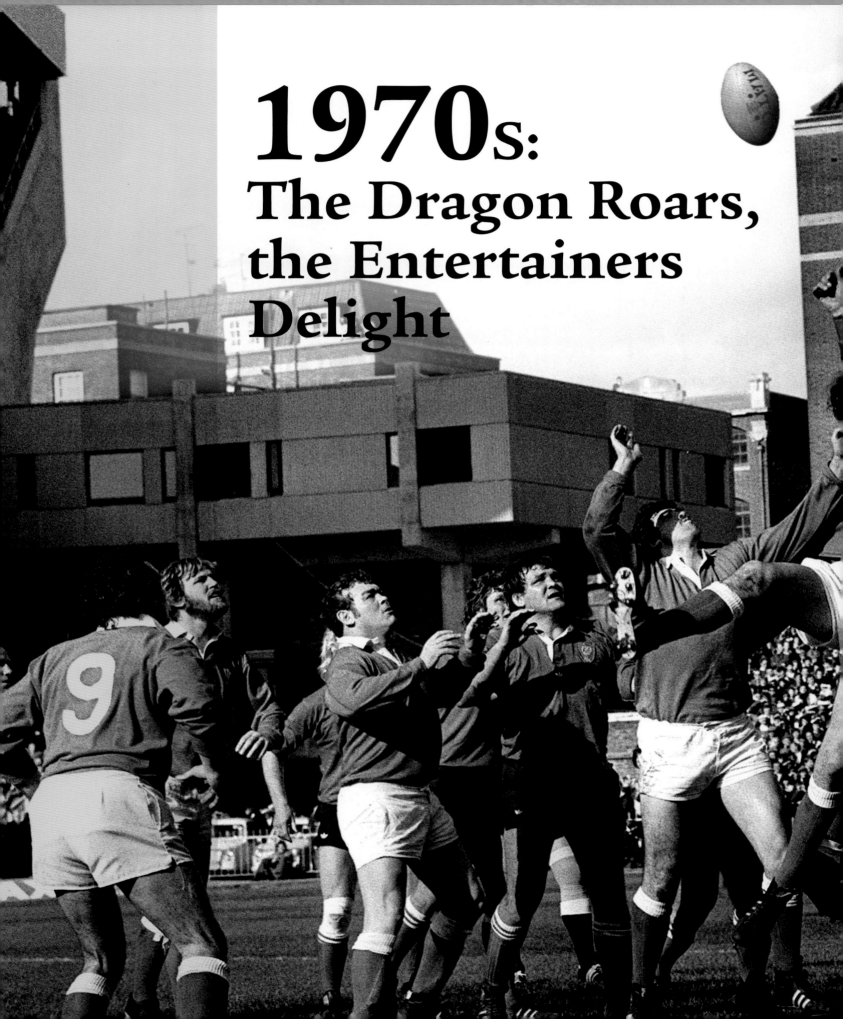

1970s:
The Dragon Roars, the Entertainers Delight

James was such a brilliant innovator as a coach, such an inspiration to those who played for him that he convinced the scratch Barbarians side that they could not only win the match but do so with a coruscating demonstration of the game's finest skills. As in 1971, a team inspired by the Welshman, delivered. Magnificently.

Yet they won, 23-11, after a blur of side steps by David Duckham, jinks by Phil Bennett, aggressive running by J. P. R. Williams and ferocious competing by the likes of Fergus Slattery, despite not having three of the key men who had played a huge part in the Lions' triumph eighteen months earlier. Barry John had gone, absurdly early, into retirement, Gerald Davies had pulled a muscle and Mervyn Davies had flu.

There was another disruption, too, before the start. When Gerald Davies withdrew, his fellow Welshman John Bevan was called in. Duckham had been chosen on the left wing, his position for the Lions in 1971 in New Zealand, but Bevan insisted he would only play on the left wing. Thus, Duckham had to switch to the right where, as he said later, 'I had the game of my life. How ironic was that?'

The tries and the manner in which they were scored that day in Cardiff should have lit a whole series of beacons around the British Isles, Ireland and France as to the way forward for the game. Indeed, great conflagrations should have told the world the news; namely, that rugby union played in this style, with this adventure and attacking purpose was the greatest game on the planet, bar none. No rugby stadium would have been big enough to hold the vast throngs who would have sought to get in to see such vivid entertainment.

Not only did a cluster of some of the finest players ever known in British and Irish rugby come together in one era – the likes of Gareth Edwards, Barry John, Gerald Davies, J. P. R. Williams, J. J. Williams, Phil Bennett, John Dawes, Mervyn Davies, Graham Price and a solid nucleus of fine forwards – but the Welsh offered a style, a panache to be envied. They dared to challenge, dared to take risks and they were handsomely rewarded. So, too, were those who went and watched them.

It is no exaggeration to say that these outstanding Welsh players were the main reason the Lions made history in 1971 against the All Blacks. As David Duckham said: 'Two-thirds of the back division was Welsh and a lot of the play was instinctive. Only Mike Gibson of Ireland and myself were not Welsh. So the rest of us just played off them. It was an absolute joy to be in that sort of class.

'Gareth Edwards and Barry John were the major influences on the way we played that 1971 series. You just knew you would get the ball in time and space with them at 9 and 10. Barry was able to stand miles away from trouble because of the length and speed of Gareth's pass. And Barry always decided very quickly what he was going to do. You knew from his body language what he would do, he was that good. But it was having the time and space that made the difference.'

Similarly, Edwards, Bennett, J. P. R. Williams, J. J. Williams and Mervyn Davies were the key men when the Lions went to South Africa three years later and left the South Africans in complete turmoil.

> 'Only Mike Gibson of Ireland and myself were not Welsh. So the rest of us just played off them. It was an absolute joy to be in that sort of class.'

Opposite: Get out of my way! Gareth Edwards delivers a jolting hand-off to All Blacks fly-half Bob Burgess during the 1971 Lions tour. Even fellow Lion Mike Gibson looks sympathetic to Burgess's plight.

'It's fair to say that by 1974 the Lions back play was not as convincing as in 1971. There was a better Lions pack of forwards in 1974 but the back play belonged to the 1971 side.'

But in 1977, the Lions' attacking play behind the scrum simply collapsed. The domination of their forwards was such that the All Blacks eventually put only three forwards into their scrum, a hitherto unknown raising of the white flag and humiliation for the once feared and physical New Zealanders.

That should have given the Lions an inevitable platform for victory in the Test series, but their poor three-quarters frittered away so many opportunities that the All Blacks somehow won Tests in Wellington and Dunedin, the Lions succeeding in Christchurch in the second Test. But at Eden Park, Auckland, in the final Test, a fortunate bounce gave New Zealand a try by Lawrie Knight and a 10-9 win that won them the Test series, 3-1. Good judges all over New Zealand were almost too embarrassed to celebrate, so great had been the humiliation heaped on their Test pack. Yet their red faces were nothing compared to those of the Lions forwards who had laid all the foundations for victory, only to see it squandered. The legacy of 1971 was truly gone.

As Lions prop Fran Cotton wrote later, 'Things got so bad that if the backs managed to pass the ball all the way down the line without dropping it, it was an achievement.'

British and Irish rugby has often produced outstanding backs of pace, skill and quality. But no decade, either before or since, has seen an emergence in the same era of such world-class talent among the countries of the British Isles and Ireland. Mike Gibson was a genius of a midfield player, a visionary performer and a brilliant reader of the game. True, he lacked one quality – searing pace – but he had just about everything else. Alongside him in the 1971 Lions team was the captain, John Dawes, a superb passer of the ball, intuitive summarizer of the play and a clever tactician. With the likes of wings David Duckham, Gerald Davies and John Bevan around at that time to unleash outside them, Dawes and Gibson were the perfect pair to set up such fast, clever runners.

Then the Lions had probably the greatest half-back partnership a touring Lions party had ever taken abroad. Gareth Edwards and Barry John were geniuses, men of sublime talents. More than that, John proved himself a superb goal kicker in New Zealand in 1971 by contributing 188 points in seventeen games.

John had retired by 1974, driven to quit the game, it was said, by the ludicrous over-hype and fuss that had been created in Wales principally by his exploits for the 1971 Lions and his achievements in a Welsh shirt. John, essentially a private man, couldn't stand the fuss and walked away from the game at the ridiculously early age of 26. His was a grievous loss to the sport in the northern hemisphere. John's brilliant tactical kicking had ended the international career of the New Zealand full-back Fergie McCormack in 1971. But Wales were fortunate: when John retired,

'Things got so bad that if the backs managed to pass the ball all the way down the line without dropping it, it was an achievement.'

Previous pages: Andy Irvine of the British and Irish Lions in action against South Africa in 1974.

Opposite: Fran Cotton, his face and hair caked with mud catches his breath before a line-out at Athletic Park during the 1977 Lions tour of New Zealand.

Previous pages: Lions
room-mates J. J. Williams
and Steve Fenwick catch up
on the newspaper coverage
on the 1977 tour.

Appalling wet weather dogged
the 1977 Lions on their
tour of New Zealand, but it
didn't dampen the crowd's
enthusiasm or the competitive
nature of the Tests.

up stepped another creative inspiration, Phil Bennett, although in fairness, even
Bennett would probably agree he was no Barry John.

But the man who was key to so much achieved by the Lions in the first half of
the 1970s and by Wales until 1978 when he finally retired, was Gareth Edwards.
The 1977 Lions manager George Burrell made an oblique reference to Edwards
by admitting at the end of that losing tour: 'Had one or two players who made
themselves unavailable for the trip been on the tour, we would almost certainly have
won the Test series.'

That simplistic view overlooked several factors. Firstly, by his own admission, Phil
Bennett should probably not have been chosen as captain of that Lions touring
party. Secondly, it completely overlooked the crass failings of the Lions backs and
thirdly, it was unfair to Edwards. He had slogged his way around South Africa in
1968, New Zealand in 1971 and South Africa again in 1974 on Lions tours. He had
more than done his bit. By now married, he wanted to spend some time with his
family, which was hardly a heinous crime.

And besides, perhaps Edwards had a suspicion about what might happen on
that 1977 tour. He couldn't have foreseen the appalling, wet weather the Lions
had to endure for fourteen weeks but he might have suspected there were few

geniuses among the likely Lions backs on the trip. With the greatest respect, players like Gareth Evans, David Burcher, Steve Fenwick, Peter Squires, Elgan Rees, Brynmor Williams and Dougie Morgan were not exactly the equivalent of geniuses like Barry John, Gerald Davies, J. P. R. Williams, David Duckham, Mike Gibson, Gareth Edwards and such like at their peak. Gibson went on the tour but never got into the Test side.

Yet a creative centre like Jim Renwick, of Hawick and Scotland, who could have added so much variety to the Lions three-quarter line in 1977, was overlooked, which has always remained a mystery. David Duckham said 'I would have loved to have gone back to New Zealand with the Lions in 1977 but was out of the England team by then. Clearly, the Lions forwards won their battle but the backs let them down. Conditions were not ideal for backs and it was a very wet tour. But they were the same for both sides.'

They called it the 'Bad News' tour and it most certainly was that. But somehow, it epitomized the shattering of the aura established by the Lions of 1971. It was like a giant balloon that had been suddenly punctured. Belief in their winning ability, simply drained away. Their supremacy in the world game had flowered so splendidly yet been allowed to wither and die cruelly early.

The Way of the Welsh Dragons

The great era of the Welsh set up a magnificent decade of the 1970s for their national team in the old Five Nations Championship. In the ten years from 1970 to 1979, Wales were Champions six times and runners-up on the other four occasions. It was an astonishing tour de force by a nation that was revelling in its prolonged spell in the spotlight. Sustained throughout those years by stalwarts like Gareth Edwards and J. P. R. Williams, Wales established a winning mentality and deep inner belief that drove them to glory time and again. They had the players, both among the forwards and especially in the backs, but most of all, they had the conviction and composure of winners. They knew that most of their opponents in the Championship simply were not in their class.

The belief of many is that it was only France who challenged Wales properly in that time. True, the French gave them some ferocious battles, the Irish, too on occasions. Yet the French were Champions only twice in that era, in 1970 and 1977. Otherwise, only Ireland, in 1974 with their first Championship title since 1951, managed to break the Welsh stranglehold on glory.

What was even more encouraging from a general perspective was that the rugby played by Wales in particular and occasionally France, was spectacular. Intense, highly committed and purposeful, the players sought to expand their game whenever possible. In the latter stages of the decade, the French under the captaincy of little Jacques Fouroux put results and pragmatism before entertainment. But in 1970, for example, the French and Welsh scored twenty tries between them in the Championship. The two countries ended up level at the top of the Championship table, both with three wins and a defeat. But France were deemed winners on point difference.

England, who ended up bottom, threatened the upset of the season when they led Wales 13-3 at Twickenham in 1970, especially when Gareth Edwards went off injured. Alas for the English, a little Welshman named Ray 'Chico' Hopkins took his place and helped mastermind a pulsating comeback to give Wales a 17-13 victory.

The Grand Slam, however, eluded Wales because Ireland finished off what England had started and threatened to do at Twickenham. They led the Welsh 14-0 and, in Syd Millar's final international, held onto that advantage to deny Wales the Slam and the Triple Crown. But only for twelve months.

In 1971, Wales celebrated the opening of their new Cardiff headquarters in appropriate fashion. Their first Grand Slam since 1952 was followed by the Lions, triumph in New Zealand. Remarkably, seven players from the London Welsh club – J.P.R. Williams, John Dawes, Gerald Davies, Mike Roberts, Geoff Evans, Mervyn Davies and John Taylor – went on that historic tour. And the Grand Slam was a thrilling, nail-biting four-match adventure that went to the wire. Tries by Edwards and John set up a narrow 9-5 win over France in Paris, a match of high quality. But the best game of the season was at Murrayfield against Scotland.

The hosts led 18-14 right at the end before Gerald Davies managed to elude

A ticket stub from the 1970 England & Wales v Scotland & Ireland game.

The tale of the 1970s. There was always a spare Welshman to out-flank the English defence. Here, full-back J. P. R. Williams is freed by Phil Bennett to expose the fractured English defence.

the defence and scoot over wide out on the right. 18-17, with the conversion to come; tens of thousands of Welshmen in the ground could scarcely breathe. It was, too, a mighty tricky one from the far-right side of the field. But John Taylor, left-footed and bearded, stepped up as the coolest man in the ground to slot the kick. They called it the greatest conversion since St Paul and it kept alive Wales's dream with a 19-18 win.

England and Ireland were duly put to the sword, and the talented, multi-skilled Welsh team won their fair reward.

But a year later, trouble flared among old friends. Due to the security situation in Northern Ireland, Scotland and Wales refused to travel to Dublin to fulfil their fixtures. This was unheard of, a gross slight against the Irish and their assurances of safety and security. It was an especially painful blow for Ireland because they had already won both their away games, in France and England, and were eyeing a possible Grand Slam for the first time since 1948.

Years later, that great warrior of an Irish forward Willie John McBride wrote witheringly of that decision by Scotland and Wales. 'Qualities such as strength of character, determination and a willingness to stand up for what you believe in were at the core of what the British & Irish Lions achieved in New Zealand in 1971. Unfortunately, six months later, we in Ireland had seen a complete

A golden age for Welsh rugby. This 1972 team photograph taken before Wales's Five Nations clash with England includes J. P. R. Williams (*front-row, far left*), Gareth Edwards (*front-row, second right*) and Barry John (*front-row, third right*). Prop John Lloyd (*with ball*) was captain.

reversal of such qualities by so-called men of rugby football.

'Rugby football had lived through an awful lot in Ireland over the years yet the game had always carried on, whatever the background and however difficult it may have been. Rugby had proved itself bigger than any man of violence for it had conspicuously refused to allow itself to be intimidated by anyone, whatever their views. Imagine our feelings then when we were let down by the ... Scottish and Welsh ... administrations. It was not the players from those countries who were to blame but their governing bodies who claimed that the violence in the North might have repercussions in the South. Those gentlemen who took the decision to abandon their matches with us that year failed Ireland, failed their own countries and failed the game of rugby football.'

Strong words, but then the Irish felt aggrieved at the decision, and no wonder: thoughts of glory had been banished by their so-called 'friends' in the game.

In France, meanwhile, a petit revolution was taking place. The powerful Béziers club started dominating the French Championship in 1971, muscling aside all-comers to lift the heavy 'Bouclier de Brennu' Championship log. Béziers would win the title in 1971, 1972, 1974, 1975, 1977 and 1978. So the national selectors had the bright idea that what worked at club level could be transferred onto the national stage. For the match in Paris against Ireland in 1972, the French chose seven men from Béziers – Jacques Cantoni, Richard Astre, Armand Vaquerin, Jean-Louis Martin, Olivier Saisset, Alain Estève and Yvan Buonomo. Alas, they lost 9-14 and by the last match of the season – Wales's Grand Slam crowning in Cardiff thanks to a 20-6 win over France – the Béziers contingent was down to one.

1973 was a curate's egg of a season. Each country won its two home games but lost twice away, leaving everyone on 4 points. The Scots were said to be winners on points, but such mathematical wizardry hardly constituted a clear Championship success. England, bottom in 1970 and 1972, went to Dublin in 1973, the first country to visit after the boycott by Wales and Scotland the previous year. They were received regally, applauded onto the field at Lansdowne Road with a storm of support.

England lost the match, 18-9, but when their captain John Pullin stood up at the after-match dinner and said simply, 'We may not be much good but at least we turn up!' he brought the house down. Strong, powerfully built men stood up and roared their approval, tears of emotion in their eyes. Rugby football can do this; it can reach the inner parts other games cannot reach.

And, wouldn't you know it, the following year Ireland won their first Championship since 1951, although there was to be no Grand Slam. They did it through just two wins, with a draw and a narrow defeat in Paris (9-6) thrown in.

For the journey to France, the Irish chose a giant of a forward by the name of Moss Keane for his first cap. The former Gaelic footballer played for the Lansdowne club and was as rumbustious as a schoolground mêlée. Trouble was, big Mossie as he was known, was accustomed to a glass or two of Guinness, the black stuff worshipped throughout Ireland. Being physically large, he could handle a few of those with no bother.

What he wasn't so good at was negotiating those squirty little glasses of champagne, which they kept cunningly refilling for you so that you never quite knew how many you'd had. And by midnight after the official post-match banquet in Paris, Moss Keane certainly didn't know how many had been sunk.

Fortunately, help was at hand. His captain for the day, Willie John McBride, had decided to keep a close eye on the new cap and duly found himself with Keane somewhere near the famous Pigalle area of the city. The only problem was, despite having devoured a fine dinner, Keane was still hungry. So McBride parked him against the wall outside a kiosk and went inside for some chips.

But McBride found himself at the end of a long queue and poor Mossie found it hard to wait. Marching into the shop, he spied a sausage on the serving shelf, picked it up and walked out, a contented smile across his chops at the thought

'Rugby had proved itself bigger than any man of violence for it had conspicuously refused to allow itself to be intimidated by anyone ...'

The official programme for the 1977 France v All Blacks game.

'I think we were supposed to go to Argentina in 1973 but that tour was called off and the New Zealanders said, "Come to us." So we did, and I played in that Test match in Auckland. But for us to win it was unheard of, it was a fluke. We were absolute no-hopers for the Test but they clearly thought we'd be easy meat and we just took them on, head-on, ran at them and scored good tries. Jan Webster outplayed Syd Going at scrum-half and John Pullin, the captain, was easily the finest England captain I ever played under.

'So we won it. But there was no sign that England would build on a performance and result like that.'

Likewise when Australia went to Twickenham at the end of that year and were comprehensively beaten, 20 points to 3. Nothing changed in English rugby at that time until a young, ebullient second row forward named Bill Beaumont came on the scene in 1975. Beaumont, with the help of others, would gradually begin to turn England from perpetual losers into a side that not only proved it could win but do so with some conviction and belief.

But before that could happen, Wales and France would end the 1970s as they began it, in dominating style. France won the Grand Slam in 1977 under the Napoleonic-type captaincy of Jacques Fouroux; Wales won in 1978, which proved to be the climax and end of the great careers of Gareth Edwards, Gerald Davies and Phil Bennett.

The 1978 triumph was clinched for Wales with their 16-7 win in the Grand Slam decider against France in Cardiff. At the end of a tough, bruising and unrelenting contest, France's Jean-Pierre Rives embraced Edwards, his old foe, and smiled. 'Gareth, you old fox, you win today. But next year in Paris … big difference!'

Edwards was so exhausted he could only nod in unconvincing agreement. For the fact was, Gareth Edwards had decided to retire a week or two earlier, as he sat in the dressing room in Ireland after a titanic battle at Lansdowne Road in which Wales had just squeezed home, 20-16. 'I knew then it was time to finish; my body was telling me so,' Edwards revealed later.

The passing of an era can induce a tear or two of emotion, and Gareth Edwards had brilliantly illuminated rugby's stage for twelve long seasons. He'd played all over the world, been acclaimed everywhere for his skills and achieved all a man could achieve in his chosen sport. Including winning a very important little personal contest with Jean-Pierre Rives, one night in Paris.

They'd celebrated long and hard, old friends together after their usual full-blooded contest on the field. And the drinking had carried on far into the Paris night. At some point, Edwards's host, the genial Rives who wasn't used to consuming great amounts of alcohol, decided they should head for another location to continue the evening's celebrations.

Thus, by complete coincidence, three Welsh supporters making their weary way home to their hotel in the small hours were suddenly approached by a Parisian taxi that, without warning, screeched to a halt. The door burst open and out stumbled France's captain who was clearly feeling much the worse for wear. Rives lost his

Opposite: David Duckham making one of his exhilarating runs. Here, he takes on Billy Steele of Scotland.

footing as he fell onto the pavement, almost at the feet of the boys from the valleys.

Concerned at his pal's plight, Edwards quickly stepped out of the taxi himself to help up his friend. At which point, one of the Welsh fans said, 'Well done, Gar. We might 'ave lost the game but we've won the drinking contest, then.'

1979 ended the decade as it had begun, with France and Wales fighting it out for the title. Wales won it again, but their 14-13 loss to the French in Paris meant no Grand Slam. Ireland finished third and bid farewell to the great C. M. H. Gibson.

France's power up front, which had been a feature of these years, was a lesson not lost on England. At last, the 'white tornadoes', as some sarcastic wag had dubbed them, roused themselves and began to discover a pack of forwards in their midst: the likes of Bill Beaumont, Roger Uttley, Fran Cotton, Mike Burton, Nigel Horton and Tony Neary. Their coming together, reflected in England's two wins out of four in 1977 and 1978, was to presage a dramatic revival of English fortunes.

The French had fielded some massive packs during the course of the Seventies. Players like Jean-François Imbernon, Michel Palmié, Robert Paparemborde, Gérard Cholley, Alain Paco, Jean-Claude Skrela, Jean-Luc Joinel, Jean-Pierre Bastiat and others had given the French a steely edge up front that few, apart from the Welsh team, could handle.

Mind you, you had to be careful when you went near those boys, on or off the field. Palmié was subsequently banned from international rugby after he had blinded a player in one eye with a finger, coming through from the

Wales's Gareth Edwards kicks for touch in their 1978 Five Nations match with France.

second row of the scrum. Cholley was a former boxer not averse to demonstrating some of his old pugilistic skills and Imbernon, the Perpignan lock, was simply a massive man. He broke his leg in one match at Parc des Princes, and was carried away to hospital. No matter, many hours later, Imbernon returned to his friends' side, his leg encased in plaster. The only problem was that a young English rugby writer was also with the French that night in the darkened nightclub. Honestly, you could hardly see your hand in front of your face. Shapes loomed up in the darkness and disappeared so what the hell hope had you when the 6 ft 6in, 18 stone Jean-François Imbernon stretched his plastered up, broken leg halfway across the room. I felt a sudden impact, followed by a roar of pain from the great bear of a man. You wonder for your own physical safety at such moments.

In general, few northern hemisphere sides could trouble the All Blacks. Scotland lost to them in 1972, 1975 (on an Eden Park pitch that was shin-deep in water after 8 inches of rain had fallen inside 24 hours), 1978 and 1979. England were beaten in 1973, 1978 and 1979, Wales in 1972 and 1978. Ireland succumbed in 1974, 1976 and 1978, but in 1973 they held them 10-10 in Dublin. To this day, it was the closest the Irish have ever come to beating New Zealand. And for those who believe the legend of Munster rugby club was born with the Heineken Cup which they won in 2006, think again. 1978 was Munster's finest day when the mighty New Zealand All Blacks were humbled. It was a day never to be forgotten in Irish rugby history.

But in 1979, six years after the great Barbarians game, there came another spectacular, memorable match in which a northern hemisphere side finally laid its All Blacks bogey to rest.

France had never won a Test match on New Zealand soil and that unhappy trend continued when they went down 23-9 at Christchurch in the first Test of their 1979 tour. They'd already lost two provincial games by that stage, and those familiar Gallic shrugs, which suggest indifference and a wish to be somewhere else, were starting to appear.

But French history is littered with tales of great deeds inspired by special men. Names such as Napoleon, Lafayette, Moulin, Le Clerc and Fouroux are legendary in a variety of French circles and now came another to earn admission to this prestigious elite. Jean-Pierre Rives seemed at times extremely laid back, but when the moment came, he could be the very epitome of inspiration. Thus, the Stade Toulouse flank forward gathered his men about him in readiness for the final match of their tour, the second Test against the All Blacks in Auckland.

The New Zealanders, silly chaps, had arranged the game on a certain date. Clearly, its importance meant nothing to them at the time but to the French, it meant everything. The match was played on 14 July 1979: Bastille Day.

In honour of those brave men and women who had revolted against oppression exactly 190 years earlier, France's rugby men similarly rose up to throw aside years of subjugation. The All Blacks found refreshed opponents confronting them, players who looked twice the performers they had done in the first Test.

In truth, the French touring team had a varying collection of talents. But in forwards like Paparemborde, Dintrans, Joinel and Rives himself, plus some fleet-footed backs who could run like the wind, weave like a fence in a gale and skip as elusively and with the charm of children, France still had plenty to offer. The difference was that Rives, their talisman, their great totem pole, had convinced them this day of French glory could be magnified by a French rugby team making history against the best side in the world. And so it came to pass.

The French attacked from the unlikeliest of situations, scored tries, kicked their goals and won 24-19. History had been made on Bastille Day; all France celebrated. At the heart of the performance had been the extraordinary Rives. That esteemed New Zealand rugby writer Donald Cameron wrote: 'All the time, Rives was hurtling about, setting up the maul here, tackling there, his hair like a beacon for the others to follow.' Rives was that quintessential Frenchman: a touch of laziness, disinterest and nonchalance mixed into one. But when the moment arrived, such torpor vanished, as if a ghostly creation. Then, this human bundle of energy, commitment, desire and dedication would invade the familiar frame. His close friends would often wonder at the paradox of the two characters that seemed to live within the one mind.

> 'All the time, Rives was hurtling about, setting up the maul there, tackling there, his hair like a beacon for others to follow.'

In the southern hemisphere, the spectre of apartheid had become an increasingly unpalatable stain upon the land of South Africa, in most people's minds except the nation's dictatorial white rulers. As the world clamoured with a growing vehemence for the release of Nelson Mandela and his colleagues, so entrenched, frightened men chose not to address the situation. It meant that sporting links with the country were becoming increasingly difficult.

Even in 1974, the British & Irish Lions only departed for their tour against a background of fierce debate and significant protest. One player, the Welsh flanker John Taylor who had been on the 1971 tour of New Zealand, refused to be considered for the tour, a commendable act of courage and conviction that put him several years ahead of most of his colleagues.

The All Blacks could tour the Republic but the Springboks did not visit New Zealand once during the 1970s. They hadn't been there since 1965 and apart from their ill-fated tour in 1981, they wouldn't go again until 1994.

Thus, just two Test series were played in that time between the world's greatest rugby-playing nations. Those tours by New Zealand, in 1970 and 1976, both resulted in 3-1 Test series wins for the South Africans. Yet the outcome of both had been in doubt at kick-off in the final Test of both series. In each case, Ellis Park, Johannesburg witnessed some extraordinary dramas. In 1970, South Africa, 2-1 up in the series, sneaked home 20-17 and six years later, with the Springboks holding an identical lead after winning the third Test, they managed an even tighter victory, 15-14, in the last Test.

A commemorative brochure for the 1970 All Blacks tour of South Africa.

ALL BLACKS
IN
S.A.

1970

An Official Publication 25c

Both series were fine contests, yet the shadow caused by South Africa's repugnant white regime hung over the occasions. As other sports isolated South Africa for its stand, rugby dragged its feet, studied its navel and did next to nothing. As it has done too often in its long life.

Of course, events of the 1980s would change all that, for all time. But what few had foreseen was that a third southern hemisphere rugby-playing nation would seize the limelight in the next decade. Even the two traditional powers in that part of the world would be forced to look to their laurels as that young, vibrant nation strode with typical confidence onto the world rugby stage.

Two of the greatest characters French rugby has ever known: The late and inimitable Jacques Fouroux (*left*) passes the ball watched by the great Jean Pierre Rives in a match against England at Twickenham.

Jean-Pierre Rives
France 1975–84
Flanker

He became a legend in French sport, revered by his countrymen for his deep love of the game and friendships rugby afforded. He was not big but as brave as a lion, a point proved when he played a Test match against Australia in 1981 with a dislocated shoulder. Representing Stade Toulouse and then Racing Club, Paris, he won 59 caps for France between 1975 and 1984 and led his country on thirty-four occasions.

'When I look back and reflect on my career, it is as though everything was a dream. It was a fantastic, magic time of my life. The people in rugby were wonderful, the players I met became friends. It was incredible. Then one day you wake up and think, "This must have been a dream."

My life was not planned to become a rugby player. I was watching television one day and saw a match and decided I wanted to play this game. It began from there, in very simple circumstances.

I enjoyed everything so much about the game: those were truly special times. Jo Maso and Walter Spanghero, two of France's greatest ever players, were my heroes when I was young. Then, one day, I played with them. Can you imagine the pleasure that gave me?

All the players in that era were really lucky because we had so much fun together. Sure, there was not money like today but money cannot buy those friendships. We enjoyed each other's company through rugby, we met all types of people in the game and saw countries all over the world. That is a great opportunity in your life.

Never forget the value of friendships. Rugby was the story of a ball with some men. But when the ball disappears the men are still there and that is the story of humanity, friendship and brotherhood.

But some things have changed. French rugby was a big mess at that time. We never knew what we were doing and that was why we were dangerous. We were

Opposite: Jean-Pierre Rives. A human bundle of energy, skill, desire and dedication.

Jean-Pierre RIVES

never predictable and teams did not know what to expect from France. I remember my great friend Serge Blanco. Nobody knew where he was going on a field, even himself. Nobody knew what he would do next. It was just a game, a very special game, but we played it with our friends to have fun together.

The game gave us great friendships but also great bruises! There were some very tough matches, especially in the French Championship. For the first 15–20 minutes of every match you tried to stay on your feet. You didn't want to go on the floor; it could be very dangerous.

Most of the rules were controlled by the players on the field. I don't know if that was good or not. But it was a game of contact and yes, sometimes a game of fighting. But I feared if you put out the fight you took away a lot of the passion.

In that time, you had your opponent and he would be there for the full eighty minutes. That was the time you knew you had to battle him. Sometimes it took you seventy minutes to win that little war against him. But now, players start a match, they try to intimidate an opponent and then they are gone by half-time or just after. Then a new player comes on.

There was a very special relationship between the French and Welsh players at that time. We had some hard matches against Wales, very hard. But there was respect, too. Players like Gareth Edwards became friends, and they still are.

Rugby has become cleaner, that is certain. But it has lost much of the drama it always had and I regret that. It is now a modern sport with no more fighting, no more wars between teams. Totally different. The fighting of the French forwards has ended but maybe they have killed the dream, too. Now, everything is neat, everything is planned. But the French are not very good at this because we follow our hearts as people. We are good when we do unexpected things. I like that.

I enjoyed the game when the outcome was unclear and the method was unknown to anyone. I don't want a pre-arranged match.

I confess, I do not like some of the modern rules. The one that allows players to hide the ball from opponents (the rolling maul) and stay in the middle of a group of players just edging forward a yard or two at a time is absurd. You are not allowed to tackle these players because you concede a penalty. But if you are not allowed to tackle, you don't have real rugby any more and that is stupid.

Keeping the ball among the forwards in that method is not exciting, just boring. It also means players do not pass the ball freely. But rugby is surely about passing the ball. It is about magic so that when you see a game with a lot of passes, it is exciting.

In my view, we have to change the rules before the rules change the game forever, change the people and their minds. Players today are very good, very fit and very clever. It could be fantastic again. But we need to free the game from these bad rules. We need to return to a game where the guy with the ball is in charge. He should have to pass the ball to keep it alive. Otherwise, a player just keeps the ball, takes a tackle, the ball takes forever to come back and it is boring.

The All Blacks are still playing in their usual way. They play very well but they play like they did. However, other countries have changed too much.

I still love rugby but perhaps most of all, my idea and my memories of it. If you are lucky, you can play this game at any time and it is a dream, a special game. I was lucky to play at a fantastic period of time and we had incredible lives. People say friendships are no more in rugby but I don't accept that. I am sure that in twenty years time this generation of players will be saying the same thing. That is the magic of rugby.

Jean-Pierre Rives demonstrates his strength and flair as he breaks through the English lines.

Gareth Edwards

Wales 1967–78
Scrum-half

Gareth Edwards became the most famous player of his time. Strong, quick, skilful and fiercely determined, he forged memorable half-back partnerships with Barry John and Phil Bennett that lit up Welsh and British and Irish Lions teams of his era. He still holds the Welsh record for the most consecutive Tests, all fifty-three from 1967 to 1978.

'What is most satisfying to me now when I look back on my career is the pleasure that other people seem to have had out of it. Their comments about those days and the matches we played for the Welsh or the Lions are a wonderful reminder of what was a very special time for all of us.

We thoroughly enjoyed ourselves playing sport. Welsh rugby was at its dominant best and I think people today can stand back and say "Yes, those were good times for rugby and for Wales." There seems to be no let up in the enjoyment people take from those memories. And I don't mean just the Welsh, but the Irish, English and Scots, too. What the Lions did in those years was special.

But I don't look back and think of it as, 'We were this or that'. It was just that we were young, we were playing to win and for the pure enjoyment. It wasn't your career, it was a release from work. And it wasn't just an enjoyable period of time but a successful one, too.

If you asked me what has best stood the test of time I'd say the friendships, the camaraderie we achieved out of it all. I still remember the good matches and whether we won or lost, but mind you, the disappointment of defeats lasted a lot longer than the wins.

When you analyse those times, I certainly think it's fair comment to say that attitudes changed from 1968 to 1971. In fact, they did so dramatically. People were far more aware of what was going on by then and remember, too, the law preventing kicking directly into touch except inside the 25, had helped open up the game enormously. It became very attractive, but there was also a greater emphasis on winning among the northern hemisphere countries.

Opposite: Edwards's was Wales's youngest ever captain, leading his country at the age of 20 against Scotland in 1968. He also possessed some hidden talents, such as the ability to do standing backward somersaults and once eating fourteen steaks in one sitting.

Gareth Edwards

The Olympic ideal is chiefly to take part but winning was always very much the focal point in the southern hemisphere. By the end of the 1960s and after those three successive losing Lions Test series people were starting to say, why do we send good players but don't win? That led to a different attitude by the administrators and players from future generations. We had been a team full of great individuals that never played as a team. But after 1968 we began to take things much more seriously. We had taken notice of the southern hemisphere approach.

The 1971 tour created such a stir because the Lions won. We had a very good coach (Carwyn James), a man who understood and read the game. He was a great man manager, too, and wasn't afraid to ask his senior players how to succeed and learn from their experience.

People have often asked me why the northern hemisphere didn't maintain the supremacy it established over the southern hemisphere in the first half of the 1970s. Well, we became stronger in the forwards, our scrummaging was stronger than theirs. So we tended to adapt and change and put a greater focus on that. In 1971, we only got 30–40 per cent of the ball and played an adventurous style because we could never control the game up front. We weren't in charge in the forwards.

But in 1974 because we were so much in charge up front, the logic was, rightly or wrongly, when we won the ball we would use it but not give it away. I remember saying, if we use all this ball, they will bash us down and seize the loose ball. So we had to be a little more careful and probably didn't have the cavalier attitude and approach of 1971. So I suppose there wasn't the same sense of adventure.

In 1977, the Lions were within a whisker of winning the series until that last-minute debacle. As for George Burrell (Lions manager) saying they'd have won the series if a couple of leading players had made the tour, well, I don't know to whom he was referring. But if one of them was myself then I take that as a compliment.

Perhaps what some people don't know is that the Lions tried to get me out to New Zealand for the final week of that tour. They had injuries and wanted me to go. But I had done no preparation at all. And my original reason for not going wasn't a rugby decision.

What people forget in today's professional game is that we held down jobs then. But for the generosity of our employers, we wouldn't have been able to play the amateur game at that level. My boss paid for me to go to South Africa twice and New Zealand once on Lions tours. In 1977, I felt I just couldn't ask again, it wouldn't have been fair. Also, I was married with a young family and I felt my family was more important to me by then than another rugby tour. I'd been there before and done it all.

And I've never regretted not going in 1977. I often think, what if I had? But I always come back to my original decision and that itself is testimony to having made the right decision in the first place.

My overall memories of that time? I feel so fortunate to have experienced all that. What you realize in sport is that there's a very fine dividing line between success and failure. We were not only fortunate in Wales and with the Lions to enjoy success but we played in an era where there was a certain style of rugby. And no one should think the exciting young players who strode the stage at that time only came from Wales. That isn't true. Look at the likes of David Duckham in England, Mike Gibson and Fergus Slattery in Ireland, Andy Irvine in Scotland. It was a very exciting era all round and I'll always feel grateful for the opportunity and good fortune to have been a part of it.

During Gareth Edwards's era the Welsh side dominated the Five Nations Championship, winning the title seven times, including three Grand Slams.

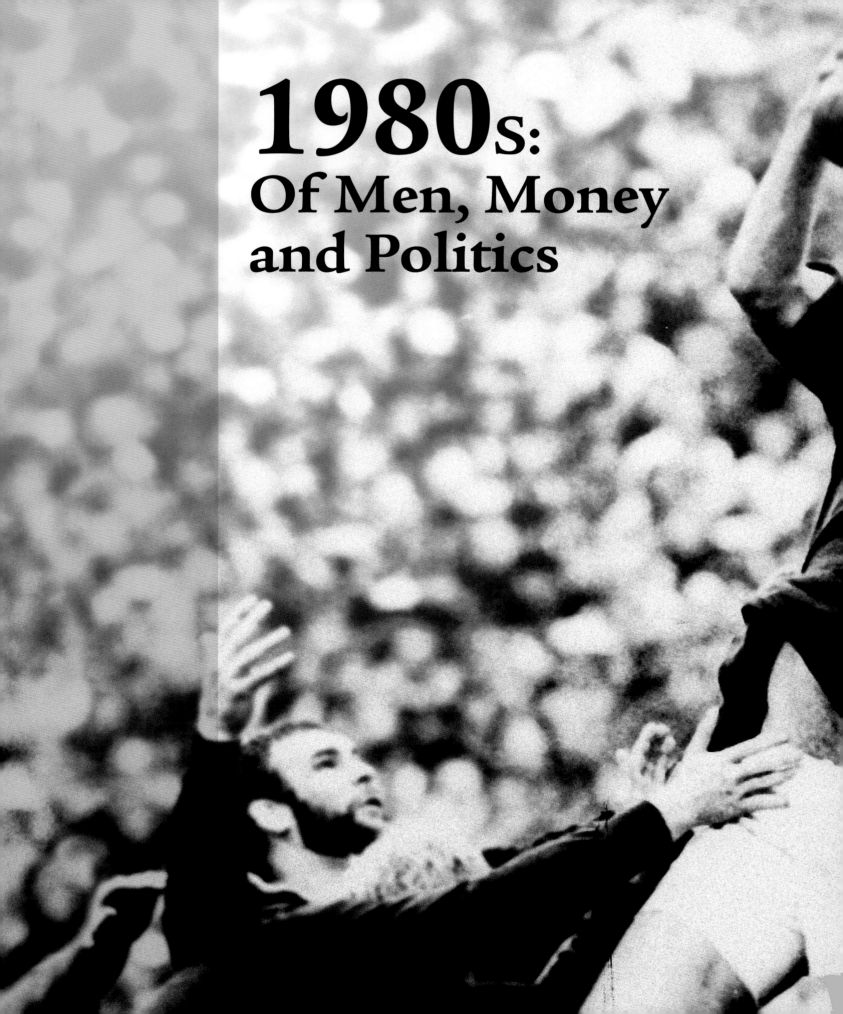

1980s:
Of Men, Money and Politics

1980s: Of Men, Money and Politics

Australia had been playing the British Isles and Ireland since 1899, France since 1928, South Africa since 1933 and New Zealand since 1903. So you could hardly say Australian rugby arrived in the 1980s.

Mind you, of the sixty-eight Test matches they'd contested with New Zealand from 1903 to 1979, the Australians had won just fifteen against the All Blacks' forty-nine. But it would be crass to ignore the Aussie boys of 1949 for their dramatic series win over the All Blacks in New Zealand.

Nevertheless, the 1980s was the decade when the Wallabies took the rugby world by storm. And some storm it was. They kicked off the era in fine style, winning a Test series at home against New Zealand for the first time since 1934. A record crowd for a rugby union game in Australia, some 48,698, poured into the Sydney Cricket Ground to see the All Blacks beaten 26-10, a result that gave the Wallabies the series by two Tests to one. That success set up a barnstorming period for Australian rugby in which they captivated the world with their stylish, innovative play and gave all manner of problems to their opponents. Frankly, their rugby was like a breath of fresh air.

'Just a few minutes listening to him and you'd want to lace up your boots, put your kit on and get onto the field. He was incredibly motivating.'

As with the Welsh in the Seventies, a uniquely talented collection of players came together to lift Australian rugby to the peak of the world game. The names of the finest have been well documented: Mark Ella, David Campese, Andrew Slack, Roger Gould, Steve Tuynman, Andy McIntyre, Simon Poidevin, Paul McLean, Tom Lawton, Nick Farr-Jones, Michael Lynagh, Michael Hawker, Steve Williams, Steve Cutler, 'Topo' Rodriguez and more.

But Australia brought something else to the party, a factor that was uniquely their own. In coaches like Bob Templeton, Bob Dwyer and Alec Evans, they had men of rugby steeped in knowledge of the game. And in the mercurial, unconventional Alan Jones they had a true professional and motivator par excellence, a man of wisdom and cunning who could probably have lifted people out of the cemetery with his powers of oratory. The England fly-half of the Eighties, Rob Andrew, spent a season in Sydney club rugby and talked often with Jones. 'Just a few minutes listening to him and you'd want to lace up your boots, put your kit on and get onto the field,' Andrew said later. 'He was incredibly motivating.'

These men urged, cajoled and inspired Australian rugby to its finest era. Within eleven years, Australia would banish humiliating memories of being lightweight opposition, a country where the British & Irish Lions could stop off en route to New Zealand and play a couple of gentler, warm-up Test matches before the real business end of the tour began across the Tasman Sea in New Zealand. More than

Previous pages: Springbok Hennie Bekker, jumping with the ball, gets a lift from team-mate Okkie Oosthuizen and Burger Geldenhuys during the controversial third Test at Eden Park in September 1981 against New Zealand.

Opposite: Australia's Mark Ella hands the ball off as he is tackled.

A brochure for the controversial 1981 Springboks tour to New Zealand.

Opposite: In one of the darkest days in rugby history, a light aircraft dive-bombs the field during the third Test between New Zealand and South Africa at Eden Park in 1981. In other fly-pasts, flour bombs were dropped as part of the protest against the 1981 Springboks tour of New Zealand, one of which injured an All Black player.

Ireland and Wales. Overall, they lost five and drew another four of their twenty-four matches, a record of unimaginable modesty for the pride of South Africa.

Not without good cause were the rugby authorities of the British Isles and Ireland known for their dinosaurial traits. They had insisted the tour should go ahead, but it did so only with great difficulty and in circumstances that reflected poorly on the game. When it was finally over, those in senior office were prodded to see sense at last by their government. It would be twenty-three long years before South Africa appeared at Twickenham again, twenty-four years before they went to Cardiff, twenty-five years before they visited Murrayfield and twenty-eight years before they returned to Lansdowne Road.

In fact, South Africa were wanted hardly anywhere. The Australians didn't see them from 1971 until 1993 and most countries of the world felt likewise. However, to their shame, countries like England, New Zealand, France, Ireland, the 1980 British & Irish Lions and the 1986 New Zealand Cavaliers, the latter little more than an allegedly money-making outfit, scuttled off furtively to the Republic in a selfish gesture that said as much about them as their desperate hosts. So, too, did a South American combined team, playing them in the Republic in 1980, 1982 and 1984 and inviting them back, to those renowned world rugby venues of Montevideo, the Uruguayan capital, and Santiago, in Chile, for two games. That South African rugby had come to this, an increasingly desperate trawl around the world to find anyone still prepared to play them, said everything about the plight to which their brutal government had subjected them.

There was one exception to the rule, where an overseas country still wanted the representatives of the white apartheid government in their midst. In 1981, New Zealand's blinkered rugby officials decreed that the South Africans were welcome to tour their country.

Rugby observers in the northern hemisphere who had ever taken the trouble to look out of their own backyard and, more especially, travel to other parts of the world, shook their heads in amazement when the New Zealand RU announced the tour would go ahead. They thought they had a pretty good idea of what would happen and it duly did. To this day, some of the scars remain sore.

If you were happy watching a rugby match from behind a barrier of barbed wire or looking on as some 3,000 protestors stormed the fences and rushed onto the field and if looking skywards as a light aircraft buzzed the ground, dropping packets of flour turned you on, then the 1981 tour of New Zealand was the place to be. But for fair-minded people, who were dismayed that rugby football could be the catalyst for such open hostility and violence and the cause of such social disharmony, it is regarded as one of the darkest chapters in the game's history. But it came about because some of rugby's authorities, refused to acknowledge the realities of (then) modern-day life and the forces for social change that were sweeping the world.

The New Zealand RU ignored obvious indications that the tour would lead to trouble. And rugby was lagging miles behind other sports in even considering extending sporting links with the odious apartheid regime back in the Republic.

South Africa had been barred from the Olympics as far back as 1964 and the Basil D'Oliveira affair of 1967 had poisoned cricketing relations. To its shame, New Zealand rugby simply ignored all these things and insisted all was well. That it chose to continue to be associated with the regime in Pretoria through sporting links was a stain on its reputation that would linger for decades.

But when the South Africans arrived in Auckland on 19 July 1981 for their tour, it's safe to say that both they and their hosts were taken aback by the scale and fury of the protests. Their match at Hamilton was called off when 350 protestors swamped the ground just before the start and police took an hour to throw out just fifty of them. Then reports swept the ground that a light aircraft had been hijacked and could be going to crash into the stands. Meanwhile, rugby fans fought with protestors. Later, the scheduled game against South Canterbury at Timaru was cancelled due to police fears that the ground would be impossible to defend.

The next week, there was a sit-down protest in one of the streets in the heart of the capital, Wellington. Peaceful protestors including women were baton-charged by harassed police, while some protestors clearly hijacked the protest to cause their own mischief for other reasons. New Zealand was approaching serious civil disorder.

Somehow, the tour limped on, doing untold damage to New Zealand's worldwide reputation and its own internal harmony.

New Zealand won the first Test, 14-9, in Christchurch but were then hammered 24-12 by the Springboks' revamped team in the second Test at Wellington. Of the provincial teams, only the Maoris could hold the tourists, drawing 12-12 in Napier.

Every other game was won by the South Africans, with the crucial exception of the third and final Test in Auckland. But the match was played out against such absurd scenes and the protests outside the ground were so furious and violent, that rugby came a distant second in terms of interest to all but the blinkered. Flares were hurled across the ground, a light aircraft made dangerously low sorties over the stadium and dropped its flour bombs throughout the game, one of which flattened the All Blacks prop forward Gary Knight.

The two sides reached the end of eighty minutes level at 22-22, the Springbok wing Ray Mordt scoring a hat-trick of tries. But the Welsh referee Clive Norling then played on briefly to cover the time lost when play was halted by the protests. In that short period, South Africa were penalized for a technical infringement and New Zealand full-back Allan Hewson kicked a long-range penalty to win the Test and the series.

But only the blind or the foolish could focus on the rugby. Too much damage had been done to New Zealand's and rugby football's reputations to bother about the games.

You'd have thought that might just have been enough of rugby's links with apartheid South Africa, that the game should have come to its senses. Alas, not so. Shamefully, just as Ireland had done in slipping into the Republic earlier in 1981 for a short tour, England then unbelievably went to South Africa in 1984 for a tour.

Opposite: South Africa's Gerrie Germishuys kicks the ball ahead during a match against Auckland at Eden Park. This controversial tour split New Zealand opinion and cast a shadow over All Black rugby.

The programme for the 1987 Australia v New Zealand game at inaugural World Cup.

18-9. But that autumn, five months later, the All Blacks set out on a tour of France. One of the matches was destined to go down in history.

New Zealand beat the French at Toulouse in the first Test and seemed certain to do so again a week later in the second Test. But French coach Jacques Fouroux, who had seen his forwards outplayed in Toulouse, inspired them to such an extent that seven days later they took on the All Blacks in a fearsome physical encounter at Nantes. The match became known forever as 'The Battle of Nantes'.

It isn't every day you pass a medical room, glance in and see a rugby player having his scrotum stitched up. That was the fate of one All Black; most others were battered and smashed to pulp by the pumped up French. France won 16-3 in a match that would prove to be a preview of the following year's World Cup final.

To say the World Cup was planned would be a touch disingenuous. It was forced on the game's hapless administrators, the then largely ineffective IRB, by commercial sharks circling the sport and spying considerable encouragement and enticement from players. For the union's amateur cat was out of the bag and all but gone. When northern hemisphere rugby men arrived in New Zealand in 1987 for the inaugural World Cup, professionalism wasn't so much as obvious as thrust in their faces. New Zealand captain Andy Dalton, who was to miss out on leading his country in the tournament because of injury, was to be seen advertising a tractor on TV. The suits from the IRB wrung their hands in silent fury, knowing full well their impotence at such blatant disregard for the laws of amateurism in the southern hemisphere.

Stories, although of course never proven, of players who were prepared to play on rebel tours of South Africa for financial reward, were equally rife. And Australia was set fair on a similar course. Meanwhile, players in the northern hemisphere like the great Welsh outside-half Jonathan Davies were still being forced to turn professional to earn money, and others were being banned forever for writing books and taking the money. The discrepancy between the hemispheres was stark and alarming.

The first World Cup was a start, not a lot more. New Zealand won it easily, because they only had one serious contest and that was the final against France, which they won 29-9. The All Blacks had blitzed countries like Italy and Fiji by 70 points or more and didn't have any serious opposition even in the quarter-final, where they beat Scotland 30-3, or the semi-final, where they thumped Wales 49-6.

The match of the tournament was a throbbing, pulsating, nerve-tingling semi-final between Australia and France. It contained six tries, huge swings in fortune favouring either side and ended when French full-back Serge Blanco finished off a sweeping move to dive in at the corner with only moments left. The French won 30-24 and Australia's great dream was over. New Zealand won a disappointingly one-sided final 29-9 against a French team that could never scale the similar heights to those it achieved in that stupendous semi-final against Australia. But equally, none could miss the supremacy and style of the New Zealanders. The All Blacks, under the shrewd, calm captaincy of David Kirk, were a smoothly oiled machine of considerable quality.

The World Cup had arrived and rugby had taken an irreversible step towards full professionalism and there would be no turning back.

Previous pages: All Black captain David Kirk goes over for a try during the 1987 Rugby World Cup Final against France. New Zealand won comprehensively 29-9.

Opposite: A battle-scarred David Kirk proudly holds-up the William Webb Ellis trophy.

Andrew Slack

Australia 1978–87
Centre

A Queenslander, he had the distinction of being the first Australian captain to lead the Wallabies to a Grand Slam on a tour of Britain and Ireland in 1984. He made his Test debut in 1978 and played for Australia until the first World Cup in 1987, by which time he had won 39 caps. He was captain nineteen times, from 1984–87. A quiet but shrewd, self-effacing man, he was not a flashy player but a team man and a popular leader.

'The only way you can properly judge an era is by consistency. OK, the Wallabies won in New Zealand in 1949 and did the odd good thing in the 1970s. But we also lost to Tonga in 1973 in Brisbane! However, in the Eighties we were consistent; no one could match that, year in year out. We won not only a large share of our games but also the really important ones. Given that we did that over a period of six to eight years, it's justified in saying things really came together for us for the first time in that period. Of course, we had some special players, which is what you need. You have got to get the right people together. But that was only one factor in the equation. There were some local issues behind it, too. One was the emergence of Queensland as a legitimate counter to New South Wales. Before that, most of the teams in Australian rugby history had been 90 per cent Sydney-based players. But Queensland established a link in the 1970s with Ray Williams, the Welsh coach, and he came out to do coaching and advise us how to go forward. Bob Templeton was responsible for bringing him out and that link began to create something and lift standards.

The other thing Queensland did was establish a relationship with New Zealand. We toured there, and they came to us which meant we were getting good, strong provincial opposition which helped us no end. Suddenly, Queensland began to emerge as a counter to New South Wales and since then there has been a balance in Australian rugby.

Andrew SLACK

Opposite: Australia captain Andy Slack breaks away, watched by England's Bryan Barley.

145

Andrew SLACK

When you add to those things a pretty good bunch of players who arrived almost together, you see why Australian rugby suddenly emerged as a serious contender on the world stage. There is always talent around but it's about that talent saying, let's keep playing, let's stick together and keep it going longer.

The two main coaches during my time associated with the Wallabies were Bob Dwyer and Alan Jones, both of whom had their strengths. But it's hard to judge completely because you can only do that if you have been in their teams for years. I played a lot for Australia in Jones's time, less so under Dwyer.

Dwyer was what you'd call an "outside the square" thinker. That had its benefits. When I had Dwyer, he was pretty naïve. He came from a club side (Randwick) that had all the superstars and he just thought that transferring all those stars to the international team would work. But of course, it didn't necessarily. The second time he was national coach, at the end of the 1980s, he was much wiser and shrewder.

They were very different personalities. Jones kept his distance from the players whereas Dwyer was much more one of the boys. I always felt Jones was more thorough. His capacity for hard work was like no others and that was contagious.

For me, Jones was the coach that changed the way Australian rugby thought about itself. I don't think there's any doubt of that. Before him, we were always comfortable with playing brilliantly at times. Our backs were great and occasionally, they'd really spark and we'd win well. But Jones was the first person who said, "That's crap. We are going to compete in every area. Not just the backs."

What Jones did in the early 1980s was make us so much more professional in the way we approached everything. There was always a clear analysis of the opposition we were going to play. A tight-head prop knew what sort of a loose-head he was going to face, our scrum-half knew all about his opposite number. Jones would have people looking at everyone. So when we went out for the match every player knew what he was facing. Jones was the one who brought in that professional preparation.

Under him, there wasn't any of the attitude of "Go out and do a bit of training and the rest of the day is yours." Even when you weren't training, Jones wanted you to be resting because he said, "You're international sportsmen: you should consider resting as part of your proper preparation for a match." It took an adjustment on the part of the players to get used to all that and there were difficulties with it. But we weren't stupid, we could see we were getting the results out of it. The methodology was producing the results. So we accepted it and mostly enjoyed it. There was great satisfaction out of winning like that and from working a lot harder than we had in the past.

I'm sure both Alan Jones and Bob Dwyer did many good, important things for Australian rugby. But would they have prospered as they both did without players like Mark Ella, Nick Farr-Jones, 'Campo', Michael Lynagh, Tim Horan and Jason Little?

They both needed quality players to achieve what they did. Yet to be fair, I always thought Jones changed the whole landscape in how the players tended to prepare, so he was the main man here.

I'd agree with the view that not winning the first World Cup was one of the biggest disappointments of my career. It left a hole in my playing record, that's for sure. I was just so disappointed we didn't get to the final, that's the thing that annoys me most about my rugby career. You have to say, we were a team past its best by then and New Zealand were the best side by far. If we had reached that final and played it ten times against the All Blacks, they'd have won eight times. But I'd like to have got there and given it a go.

For me, looking back at those years, the game had an enormous influence on my life. But it's never been my whole life, the complete package. Family means more to me than anything else. It was enjoyable playing rugby and we did have success. I had a great time at school, too. But I remember most the people that I was involved with, not the actual matches and the wins or defeats. They fade in time. But the friendships endure.

A popular team player, Andrew Slack was at the hub of the Australian rugby revolution. Here, he kicks for touch against France.

Danie Gerber
South Africa 1980–92
Centre

Danie Gerber was regarded as one of the greatest centres ever produced by South Africa. Strong, fast and powerful with a devastating hand-off, his career was ruined by the apartheid years in his country.

'I had always wanted to play against the All Blacks, especially in New Zealand. For me, they were the best in the world, the toughest side of all the rugby-playing nations. I had never been to New Zealand and wanted to experience it.

But if I'd known before I left what would happen on that tour, what it was going to be like, maybe I would have stayed at home. One thing's for sure. There will never be a tour like that again. I went just to play rugby, I wasn't interested in the political stuff. I didn't think I'd be afraid of what would happen, I just wanted to play the All Blacks.

But I was afraid, especially when we saw the aeroplane coming low over the ground at Eden Park for the third Test. It was so low that some rugby fans were throwing things at it, although they were warned not to do so. I reckoned I could have hit it if I'd kicked the ball hard enough up into the sky. It didn't seem much higher than the top of the goalposts.

We were worried the plane would get hit or collide with something and crash on the field. By half-time, we were 16-3 down because we'd played the first half facing the direction from which this plane kept coming. And it must have made fifty or sixty sorties low across the ground. When we played with our backs to it in the second half we could focus more on the rugby.

We had an instant introduction into what was going to happen when we first landed in New Zealand at the start of the tour. There were about 3,000–4,000 demonstrators at the airport and they were shouting and screaming. The bus came onto the tarmac to pick us up at the plane, but we could hear them. It was unnerving.

The tour split the New Zealand people in terms of opinion. There were problems throughout the tour and afterwards, too, in the country.

Because of the demonstrations wherever we went, we couldn't use hotels everywhere and some nights we stayed in the local cells at the police station. At least it was safe in there, if not very comfortable on the bunk beds. On other occasions, we'd bed down in the pavilion at some sports ground where they'd installed bunks.

Opposite: On account of apartheid politics Danie Gerber won just 24 caps in twelve years.

Danie GERBER

Before the first Test in Christchurch, we stayed in a building that housed squash courts. Again, we were camping out on makeshift beds and the mattresses weren't very comfortable. Often the sleeping places were cold and occasionally, we would have to go by bus to the ground at five or six in the morning to avoid demonstrators. That meant a long wait until kick-off at 3 p.m. but we did it. And at some places the New Zealanders put in entertainments for us like pool tables and they cooked us food there. A few of the pavilions became like hotels for us because the police could guarantee security there.

After the match at Hamilton against Waikato was cancelled when the demonstrators broke down fences, invaded the field and threw stones and nails onto the pitch, we were in two minds about whether we would stay or go home. Our management went for a meeting with the police to discuss it. When they got back, they told us there was good news and bad, which did we want first? We said the bad news. It was that the game at Timaru would also have to be cancelled. But the good news was, we were staying and completing the rest of the tour. There was a big roar of relief at that. But it became difficult to concentrate on the rugby. The moment you saw all those demonstrators, you were a bit worried. They were throwing eggs and stuff whenever you went to board your bus. One day, I went out of a hotel to a shop to buy some chocolate. When you went out like that, you could never wear your Springbok blazer, tie or jumper or anything that made it obvious who you were. But a lady and two guys recognized me and three other players I was with (Hennie Becker, Louis Moolman and Divan Serfontein) from photographs I suppose, and they started berating us. They were shouting, "You are racists go home, you have split our country, we don't want you here". It was pretty unpleasant and we had a lot of problems in those circumstances. The people said a lot of terrible things to us and it was quite hard to take.

What these people didn't know, and didn't want to know, was that someone like me had played with black and coloured players in invitation teams for some time. I didn't have a problem playing with them. I also coached rugby and cricket in black townships long before I was a Springbok. But people didn't want to know that. Because of the political situation the New Zealand public who criticized us thought we were against black people all the time. But I couldn't help what my government was doing.

I knew things were wrong in South Africa and that we had to change. But those decisions weren't in my hands or the hands of other Springboks. I'd hoped we would have changed before we did but the politicians did what they wanted.

However, what is also important to remember about that tour is that many New Zealanders were in favour of it. They wanted to help, and they did so by taking us out so we could enjoy ourselves. They are a wonderful people and I have nothing against New Zealanders. We were welcomed by many of them and had some great parties in their company. Perhaps it was ironic but the best party we had on that tour was after the match we'd played against the NZ Maoris. So you couldn't blame 90 per cent of the people. But I understood the views of the protestors. However, I was a rugby player, not a politician.

Could we have won that series? Well, we had our chances in the first Test, but in the final Test I certainly didn't agree with the penalty in injury time that lost us the match and the series. One of their players took a tap penalty and the guy ran at least 15 metres before we tackled him. But the referee gave a penalty and they won the series with it.

I have subsequently come to understand the allegation that it was probably set up that New Zealand had to win the series otherwise there would have been even bigger problems for them. It was important they won that match and the series. The way that last penalty was given suggested that.

Despite his limited Test career, Danie Gerber has, by ratio, the best Springbok try-scoring average, with 19 in 24 Tests.

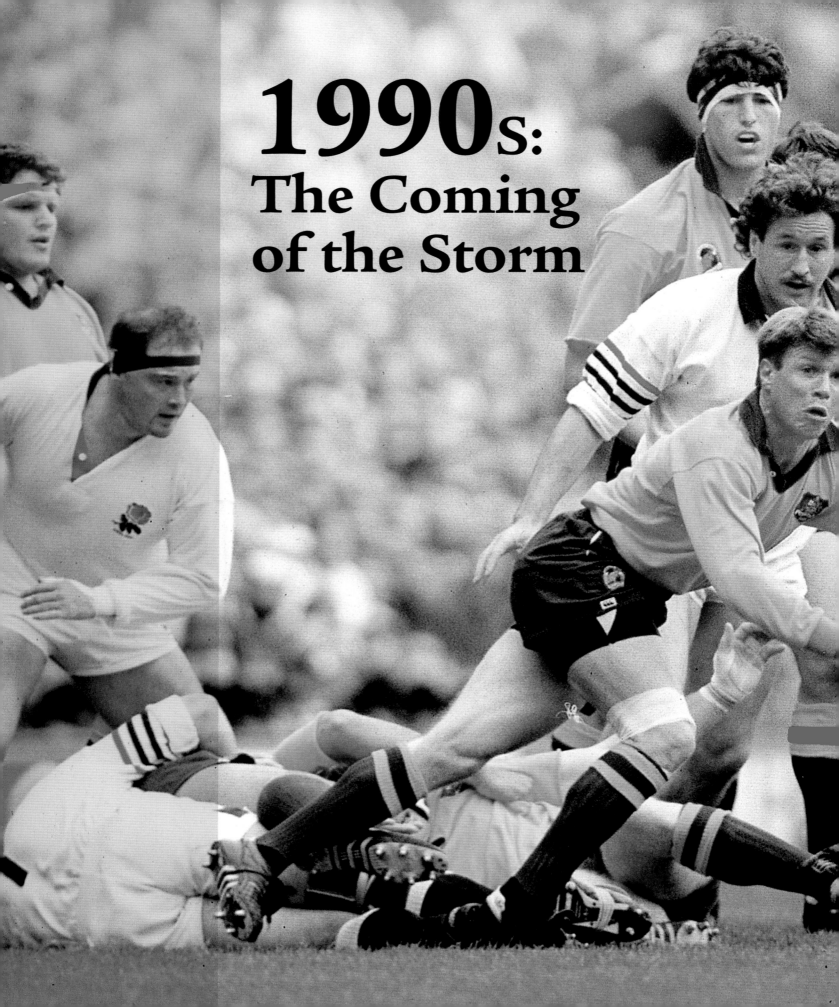

1990s:
The Coming
of the Storm

1990s: The Coming of the Storm

The 1990s was the decade that changed rugby forever. Evolution was replaced by revolution in the game.

The decade began with countries like Ireland making goodwill tours of countries like Namibia (and losing both Tests to them) and ended with most of the rugby-playing world outside the leading nations fearing the effects of professionalism. They had every reason to be concerned.

Paris on a warm August afternoon was the location for rugby union to make history. Given that the French capital had staged Europe's most famous revolution, it somehow seemed an appropriate venue.

In the modest surroundings of the Ambassador hotel in the heart of Paris, a single announcement changed the game forever. It was 26 August 1995, and the then Chairman of the International Rugby Board, Vernon Pugh, made the historic statement in just a single sentence. 'Ladies and Gentlemen, we declare that the game of rugby union is now open.'

> 'Ladies and Gentlemen, we declare that the game of rugby union is now open.'

Just two months earlier, the third Rugby World Cup had been staged in South Africa. It had been a vibrant, colourful, pulsating, controversial success. Things were moving fast in the world and rugby simply reflected that trend.

On the day before the World Cup final in Johannesburg, it was revealed that Rupert Murdoch's News Corporation had offered a sum of around $550 million for television rights to a new Tri-Nations tournament featuring Australia, New Zealand and South Africa. The genie was at last out of the bottle.

Mind you, the cap had been loosened originally, not by a commercial operator like Murdoch but, irony of all ironies, by men who swore they would defend the sport's amateur ethos to their dying day. Officers of the individual unions fiercely upheld the amateur concept on the one hand, yet at the same time invited increasing amounts of sponsors' money into the game. They could not see how one thing would inevitably lead to another.

As the sponsors clambered to get involved with a game of increasing attraction to growing numbers of the general public, the players, those who were the centre of attention, were being told, 'This money has nothing to do with you, it's for the game.'

Such a scenario was naive and absurd: it ignored the ways of the world. Not only did it create resentment in the dressing rooms of the senior game, but the increased demands from countries that their players spend ever more time preparing and playing the game to elevate standards still further, caused deeper dismay. The consequences of this state of affairs was blindingly obvious to everyone, it seemed, except those who ran the home unions in the northern

New Zealand wing John Kirwan attempts to break through the Australian defence during the 1991 World Cup semi-final match at Lansdowne Road, Dublin.

hemisphere, in countries like England, Scotland and Ireland. The Welsh had always been a tad more realistic and as for the French, well, the joke was, they just carried on paying their players.

In the southern hemisphere, far away from the IRB's home base, it was another story. Here, realism had dawned many years earlier. It was considered simply a matter of time before the whole amateur edifice collapsed. It was already cracking and crumbling. What was certain to bring it down was the advent of a World Cup, which had started back in 1987. Perhaps only a sport as conservative as rugby union could have stumbled and staggered through another eight years of denial before reality was finally grasped.

There was, in effect, a sham through the first half of the 1990s. Gala dinners to raise money for players' funds were being organized in southern hemisphere countries, where generous expenses being paid were already the equivalent of a wage. Rugby union had become professional in all but name.

The second World Cup in 1991 was hosted by the Five Nations Championship countries. This meant games were played all over Britain, Ireland and France in such widespread locations as Bayonne, Béziers, Belfast, Pontypridd, Llanelli, Leicester, Lille, Lansdowne Road, Edinburgh, Gloucester, Cardiff and Twickenham. This was casting the net too far.

But it was a tournament lit up by the dazzling back play of Australia, the eventual winners, most notably in their semi-final victory over New Zealand in

The official programme for the 1991 Rugby World Cup final Australia v England.

Dublin. The genius of David Campese was at its zenith that day; his arcing run from the unfamiliar fly-half position taking him outside the New Zealand defence for a memorable try, and his scintillating break down the right and mesmerizing flipped pass putting Tim Horan over for another. New Zealand couldn't live with that kind of brilliance.

Indeed, David Campese was dragging the old game, almost single-handedly at times it seemed, out of its amateur ethos towards the new dawn of entertainment, personality and mass media coverage. After all, 'Campo' had been visiting Italy in the northern hemisphere winters since the mid-1980s to play club rugby. It's safe to say he wasn't there just to endure the freezing Milanese winters.

Campese epitomized rugby's march towards the alluring lights of its professional future. This complex character from Australia – derided as a loud-mouth by those who didn't know him, but respected as often shy and self-effacing by those who really did, was undoubtedly the chief playing figure of his era. For entertainment, buzz and excitement, no one could match him when he got the ball. Invariably, something extraordinary would happen.

Of course, Campese made mistakes. But then, most geniuses are flawed in some respects. Study the bigger picture, the wider scenario and you see the enormous benefits. As ever, Australia's 1991 World Cup winning coach Bob Dwyer hit the nail on the head when asked once how he coached a maverick talent such as Campese.

> 'Mate, I make it a policy of mine never to interfere with bloody genius.'

Dwyer, now back in charge of the Wallabies, retorted, 'Mate, I make it a policy of mine never to interfere with bloody genius.' How right he was, especially considering the fact that Campese himself often admitted that he never quite knew which way his mind and legs would take him on a rugby field. If he wasn't certain, how could any coach make complex plans for him? Dwyer's genius was that he allowed Campese's brilliance to flow largely uninhibited. Australia won the World Cup due in large part to that fact.

England, by complete contrast, had ground their way to the final by means of a hard, physical, forward-orientated 19-10 win over France in Paris and a dour 9-6 kick-riddled game against Scotland in Edinburgh. The Paris spectacle was enlivened by the sight of the brilliant French full-back Serge Blanco punching an opponent and, later, the French coach Daniel Dubroca allegedly assaulting, the referee.

The final was played at Twickenham in front of Her Majesty The Queen. Maybe it was the presence of royalty, maybe Campese's goading remarks in the week leading up to the match. But whatever the cause, England bizarrely abandoned their focus on hard-driving forward play, which had taken them to the final (and Grand Slam in the 1991 Five Nations Championship), and attempted a glitzy, ambitious game plan based around backs who were not used to such a glut of possession in their hands. Not surprisingly, they ran the wrong lines, drifted across field incessantly, failed to break the gain line or penetrate properly, and fumbled frequently.

All this simply played into Australia's hands for the Wallabies forwards were in no way the equal of the England pack. Had England driven the ball up strongly off the

Opposite: John Eales and Tony Daley celebrate Australia's victory over England at Twickenham in the 1991 World Cup Final. The despondent England captain Will Carling can be seen in the background.

fringes, dominated first phase and kicked for position, they would almost certainly have overpowered and strangled the life out of the Australians. A World Cup final must first be won, then analysed for style marks, not the other way round.

As it was, England threw away a World Cup that was theirs for the taking. But they reaffirmed their power and quality by winning a second successive Grand Slam in the 1992 Five Nations Championship three months later.

One momentous event seemed to follow another in this decade. On 11 February 1990, Nelson Mandela had walked out of jail in South Africa a free man, to the delight of the democratic world. The collapse of the old guard in South African politics heralded a new era for the country, and also for the Springboks.

A Stranger Returns

In most countries, the long years of isolation would have meant a painful process of gradual and frustrating rebuilding. Therefore, when the Springboks reappeared on the world stage, they were horribly exposed. In 1992, they lost 33-16 to England at Twickenham and then 26-3 to the new world champions Australia in Cape Town. The critics and pessimists on the high veld forecast years of such humiliations. Yet the same year, when New Zealand went to Johannesburg, they only just sneaked home 27-24. The green shoots of a Springbok recovery could already be detected, and they were confirmed when South Africa beat France in Lyon 20-15 at the end of that first year back. France won the second Test in Paris, 29-6, to square the series but it was obvious that the pace of the South African rugby recovery was gathering momentum.

In 1994, the Springboks hosted England, losing the first Test in Pretoria 32-15, but winning in Cape Town, 27-9. It was a tour sullied by violence in the match against Eastern Province at Port Elizabeth, when Tim Rodber was sent off and Jonathan Callard had his face and eye kicked by a local player, causing twenty-five stitches to be inserted. Unhappily, the culprit got away with it.

Later that year, the Springboks returned to the northern hemisphere for a proper tour, beating Wales 20-12 and Scotland 34-10. But it wasn't just the results that mattered.

World rugby had been denuded by the Springboks' isolation. The banishment was deserved but the game in general suffered, there was no doubt of that. At a glittering reception at an elegant Scottish country house outside Edinburgh in the week leading up to the Springboks first international against Scotland for twenty-five years, kilts and tartan jackets mixed freely once again with those wearing Springbok blazers. Beside crackling log fires, it felt fantastic to all who were there the night that South African rugby had come in from the cold.

Steadily, inexorably through these early matches, South Africa was finding the core of a team for the 1995 World Cup. True, they flopped in New Zealand in 1994, in a poor series. But the nucleus was being assembled, and none could dispute the talent available. Led by François Pienaar in the back row, there were forwards of proper substance like the Natal lock Mark Andrews and renowned scrummager

Balie Swart in the front row, Chester Williams and James Small on the wings, Japie Mulder at centre and the man dubbed 'The Rolls-Royce of full-backs' André Joubert. Others, like the brilliantly talented scrum-half Joost van der Westhuizen and flanker Ruben Kruger, would be added soon.

The 2-0 Test series defeat in New Zealand with the last Test drawn cost coach Ian McIntosh and manager Jannie Engelbrecht, two of South African rugby's most revered figures, their jobs, both being dismissed by the volatile South African Rugby president, Louis Luyt. In came Kitch Christie and Morne du Plessis as coach and manager respectively. The scene was set for a South-African hosted World Cup in 1995.

To this day, it remains one of the best, surpassed only by the Australian-hosted event of 2003. The sun shone, the light was exceptional, the nation was captivated and visitors were welcomed regally (excepting the poor unfortunates who were

Scotland captain Gavin Hastings tries to power through South Africa's Ruben Kruger and Pieter Hendriks during the Springboks tour of Great Britain and Ireland in 1994.

victims of violence, mainly in Johannesburg). None who were in the Republic between the day of the first match, 25 May, through to the final on 24 June, could fail to grasp the bosom-like relationship between white South Africans and rugby football. Everywhere you went, most people you talked to had just one topic of conversation on their lips: the Rugby World Cup.

Australia, the defending champions, still had their 1991 winning coach Bob Dwyer in charge and they also retained several star players like Campese, Lynagh, Little, Horan, Eales, Kearns, Ofahengaue and McKenzie. They had added the likes of George Gregan and Matthew Burke, players who would in time become star names themselves. But the Wallabies didn't quite have it up front. They lost their opening match to South Africa, a tension filled affair at Newlands Stadium, Cape Town, by 27 points to 18 and then were felled by England in the quarter-finals, but only 25-22 because of a last minute drop goal from 45 metres by England fly-half Rob Andrew.

But one man seized the 1995 World Cup by the scruff of its neck. He wasn't English or Australian, nor even a South African. He was a New Zealander, he was just 20 years old and his name was Jonah Lomu. A physical colossus, an absolute

Rob Andrew lands the vital drop goal in the 1995 Rugby World Cup quarter-final against Australia to win the game 25-22.

freak at 6 ft 5 ins tall and 18 stone 8 lb in weight, Lomu went through the world's leading rugby nations at that World Cup like a combine harvester through a field of corn. Anything standing was razed to the ground.

He scored two tries in the All Blacks' 43-19 demolition of Ireland and if he wasn't scoring tries himself, he was making them for others. Mercifully, he didn't play when New Zealand beat Japan 145-17 in their group match. If he had, it would probably have been closer to 200.

Results such as that, and Scotland's 89-0 flogging of the Ivory Coast, revealed how weak some of rugby's lower tiers really were. The tragic accident suffered by the Ivory Coast wing Max Brito in the 1995 tournament underlined the dangers of such mis-matches.

Brito was playing for his country in their final pool match against Tonga at Rustenburg. He went to pick up a loose ball, slipped and was engulfed by the big, physical Tongan players arriving for the ball. When the ball was released, Brito was seen laying motionless on the ground. He never moved again. The young man had suffered a horrifying paralysis rendering him a quadriplegic for the rest of his life.

Brito was flown to hospital, comforted as far as possible and eventually flown back to France. One month after the World Cup had ended, I walked into his hospital room at a clinic in the suburbs of Bordeaux. There he lay, from outward appearances his lean body a testimony to his sporting fitness. But alas, he could move barely a finger, certainly not an arm. He was helpless; fed by his carers, cleaned by them and with the prospect of spending the remainder of his life in such a state.

> 'I am a man at peace with myself, I am not stressed ... I do not blame rugby for this, it can happen to anyone for the neck is so fragile.'

We talked briefly, through an interpreter, and his words were whispered, halting. The emotion of the occasion was haunting. I resolved to return at a later date. When I did, a year or more later, he had retrieved just the slightest movement in one hand, but in reality desperately little. But he had by then formulated his thoughts.

'There have been very, very depressing moments, truly black times particularly at the beginning. I believe everybody in this situation must go through that phase.

'You cross periods that are mentally very delicate and which lead you to think of suicide. It is a watershed, a necessary stage that one gets over or doesn't. It is a traumatic event in your life but you have to come to terms with it and that takes time.'

The experience gave Max Brito a perspective on life few ever encompass. 'I see people getting angry for such small, insignificant reasons. So many problems between people could be avoided. Most are really not very important anyway. When I see children dying and starving on TV and then hear people arguing about petty things, it makes me laugh bitterly. There are many hard things in life, things that need more attention.'

And his own situation? 'I am a man at peace with myself, I am not stressed,' he said. 'I do not blame rugby for this, it can happen to anyone for the neck is so fragile.'

The calm dignity and the logical reasoning he offered somehow intensified the awful sadness.

Scotland caught the full force of the typhoon known as Jonah Lomu in their 1995 World Cup quarter-final against the All Blacks. Lomu scored only one try but his powerful running and coruscating hand-offs caused chaos in the Scottish defence. It finished 48-30, respectable enough on the scoreboard, but New Zealand's 45-16 lead at one stage was a better indication of their superiority. That, allied to England's dramatic late win over Australia, paired the two nations in the semi-final. The pre-match hype and build-up was not a wasted exercise – this proved to be one of the defining games of any World Cup.

In the very first minute, Lomu picked up the ball for the first time, smashed through the attempted tackle of Tony Underwood, gathered sufficient speed to outpace the covering England captain Will Carling and then simply ran straight through and over full-back Mike Catt to score a stunning, staggering try of pace and enormous power. That single act defined the game and also decided it. England had the look of rabbits caught in a car's headlights writ large upon their faces. Even at that early stage, you knew there was no way back for them.

New Zealand finished with 45 points, Lomu with four tries and England (who somehow scored 29) with bruises all over their bodies. But the great man himself would come to regret not the tries but the fuss and adulation it created throughout the rugby-playing world. He said after the tournament, 'It is horrible to be this well known. Fame is highly overrated. I could do without it all really; it makes me feel very uncomfortable.' It was

In a demonstration of his immense power and pace All Black Jonah Lomu evades a challenge from Rob Andrew during the 1995 Rugby World Cup semi-final. New Zealand cruised to victory 45-29.

Joost van der Westhuizen feeds his backs during South Africa's semi-final clash with France.

something Lomu was going to have to learn to live with throughout his entire career.

In the other semi-final, meanwhile, South Africa had survived a Durban deluge as well as everything the French could hurl at them, to win a match played in appalling conditions.

In the event, the French went within literally an inch of spoiling South Africa's party. That was how close one of their forwards came to a touchdown that would have ended the Springboks' hopes. In the event, South Africa squelched home 19-15 and the 50,000 crowd then attempted to do likewise.

Durban airport became the focus of the entire country. Planes were lined up like buses outside a football ground. In the end, the ground staff simply couldn't cope. Allocated seats became a fantasy and when the doors of the terminal were opened leading to the planes, a rush ensued. Those first on seized the first class seats and swilled champagne all the way down to Cape Town. Flights were still arriving there at nearly two o'clock in the morning. But somehow, South Africa coped.

How the Springboks would cope in the final with Lomu and the dominant New Zealanders who had played by far the best rugby of the tournament, was

Following pages: Two great rugby superpowers line-up prior to 1995 World Cup final.

'There was an outcry, people were saying "Why are we losing games"? People were being rude to my wife of the time in the supermarket, it was extraordinary,' remembered Best. 'One guy went up to her and told her I was a w*****. She said "You tell him that yourself. But he'll punch your lights out".'

Best had been asked to go on the British and Irish Lions tour of New Zealand that summer as assistant coach to Ian McGeechan. So he flew home from Dublin with England on the Sunday morning and went straight into a selection meeting at Heathrow airport to choose the Lions squad.

In the event, the Lions lost the series 2-1 that year, but only after what they regarded as a dreadful piece of refereeing that cost them victory 20-18 in the first Test at Christchurch. They won the second Test comfortably but lost the third, heavily.

'We got cheated out of the first Test by the referee giving a penalty to New Zealand right at the end,' Best alleged. 'We blew them away in the second Test but they bounced back well in the last one. It was very disappointing; that should have been only the second Lions team that century to win a series in New Zealand.'

Best had been working for a travel company in Twickenham and his name as England coach was an undoubted attraction to them. His coaching tenure, from late 1991 to mid-1994, spanned seventeen matches of which England won fourteen, a supreme effort. Yet with the 1995 World Cup less than a year away, Best went home one evening to be told that Graham Smith, the chairman of the RFU's coaching sub-committee, was waiting for him in his living room. That wasn't a complete surprise because Smith's wife was godmother to one of Best's children. But when England's coach

'You tell him yourself. But he'll punch your lights out.'

walked into the room, he knew instantly why Smith was there. One look at his face told me, before he'd said a word. He just said the committee felt it was time for a change. 'When I look back now and think that firing was brought about because we lost two matches, I am left scratching my head.' The early 1990s had been crucial years for England. Best explained 'Geoff Cooke was instrumental in laying the groundwork for so much of what England went on to achieve. He brought a background of sports science to the game, which people had never understood and we got much better organized, although it was still technically in the amateur era.'

Within almost weeks of losing the England job, Best's old club Harlequins had stepped in to sign him up. Seeing the way the game was going, they made him English rugby's first fully paid Director of Rugby. The new era had begun.

'I thought, why not? I'd been working all hours trying to do a day job and then coaching all over the place, followed by travelling at weekends. It was a hell of a commitment. The 'Quins offer meant that I'd be paid well for doing a job I had been doing for years for nothing. It was a no-brainer, really.'

Best saw close-up the way the RFU floundered when professionalism was announced, like a bolt from the blue. 'They'd all been cocooned inside their own little private worlds; they didn't understand that this was now a potentially huge commercial sport with important business decisions to be taken. They could have signed up the best 120 players to the Union and they'd have had control ever after.

Previous pages: Ireland's hero Eric Elwood is held aloft after their historic victory over England (17–3) in the 1993 Five Nations. The victory prompted jubilant celebrations.

Opposite: British and Irish Lion's lock Wade Dooley wins a line-out in the 1993 tour of New Zealand.

David Campese
Australia 1982–1996
Wing

A mercurial character who enjoyed flouting convention and played his rugby in similar style. Won 101 caps for Australia between 1982 and 1996 and established a reputation as the most exciting, entertaining player of his generation. He remains far and away Australia's record try scorer with sixty-four tries in his century of Tests.

'Coming from a small town in Australia, where I grew up surrounded by rugby league, I just played for fun. And I tried to follow that approach throughout my career. Mind you, it was different in those days to the present time. When we went on tours in the 1980s, we had some doctors and lawyers amongst us and a few were even doing exams or preparing for them at the airports. That was why rugby was somehow more than just about sport. It was a lot more prestigious.

The Wallabies 1984 Grand Slam tour of Britain and Ireland was really special. We had a coach in Alan Jones who was ahead of his time and that was another of the reasons we won the Grand Slam. Jones was a disciplinarian and if you wanted to be in the team, you had to play to what he wanted. He would give you the info about people and expect you to deliver. But we also had some fantastic players, and they were vital. You can be the world's greatest coach but if you haven't got the players to work with, you won't win.

People in Britain and Ireland just enjoyed rugby, that was all, and we played the sort of rugby they wanted to see. They probably hadn't seen the skills we showed compared to what they were used to.

That tour was also an opportunity to travel the world and see new places. I never thought I would play rugby at the highest level or go to all those places so to be given the honour and privilege of touring with Australia was something else as far as I was concerned. I would have gone anywhere to play rugby. I just loved the game.

That tour was great because we met so many different people. And when you go back years later, you see some of them again and enjoy the friendships once

David Campese

more. To me, that was what rugby was about. Now, it's just a job for these guys; it's not what it was. And the modern players won't meet people and have a drink with them.

I found it very character building to play for the Wallabies at destinations all over the world. When you played in a provincial country town in New Zealand on a Wednesday afternoon or at Llanelli or Swansea on a Saturday, you learned so much. I came into the Wallabies side at 19 and just listened and learned. That way, you acquire the knowledge that enables you to set examples to the next generation.

It was tough at times; you had to work and train hard. But we looked forward to training then; now, it's just a job for the modern players, that's all they have to do. The Wallaby teams of that time also had a lot of leaders and that is something that has changed compared to now. You haven't got any leaders much today. But the more leaders on the field, the better team you will have.

The 1988 Australian tour of the UK wasn't as successful for the team but for me personally, it was a good one. 1988 was my best season and I played well. I felt good, felt fit and didn't have too many worries in my life. We had toured New Zealand in 1986 and won there at last, but in 1987 we failed to win the World Cup at home and copped a lot of criticism. When we came away in 1988, there wasn't as much pressure on that UK tour.

We won the World Cup in 1991 which was a fantastic thing for us. But in 1995 in South Africa, a lot went wrong. I'd gone from 82 kg to 92 and those 10 kg I put on, meant I lost a lot of my speed. Sure, I'd added bulk but lost pace. That was down to Bob Dwyer trying to get big guys in his team. But we also had four of the pack injured, that didn't help. South Africa caught us on the hop at the start of that 1995 World Cup and things had started to change. Not for the better either, in many ways.

After the game against England, Nick Farr-Jones, who was the senior player, said to George Gregan, "Come to my room and we'll talk". But Gregan never even turned up. That showed the arrogance of people and the problems we had off the field. Guys were worrying more about what was happening off the field than with the actual game. If it had been me, I'd have been the first one there in those circumstances because I wanted to learn and improve.

Professionalism was coming way back in the first half of the 1980s. I played in Italy from 1984 to 1992 and I was in effect a professional. But my attitude never changed. I just wanted to play rugby. I was there because I enjoyed rugby and my goal was to be the best possible player in my position. Sure, the Italians looked after me. But money wasn't my No. 1 target. How could it have been? I used to turn up for Barbarians games over Christmas at Leicester and stand around for hours after signing autographs. I never minded; it was always great to play. But you wouldn't get players doing that now. When the Barbarians play these days, the players get £5,000 each. And they play rubbish rugby.

I continue to believe that even now, if you had a player who combined work with his rugby, he would be a lot better as a player because he would have more things on his mind than just rugby. Unless you are really dedicated not just to be a player but to be the best player in the world in your position and your mind is fresh and focused, then a mixture of professionalism and amateurism would probably suit most guys.

To me, being a professional player is not about money, but attitude. If you haven't got the attitude, it doesn't matter how much money they give you. The best players have always had the best attitude. What was it Gary Player said, "It's a strange thing but the harder I practise, the better I get."

'I never quite knew where my legs were going.' David Campese in action against the Barbarians in 1984.

François Pienaar
South Africa 1993–96
Flanker

François Pienaar had a comparatively short international career for South Africa, from only 1993–96, but he was captain for every one of his 29 caps and is best known for being an inspirational leader and captaining the Springboks to the 1995 World Cup.

There can be no better feeling for a rugby player than to win the Rugby World Cup. But perhaps in a wider sense there can be a more important element attached to that achievement. The feeling was that our nation came together in the light of that World Cup and South Africa's triumph for the first time in total harmony and rejoicing. By anybody's standards, that was some success in an altogether wider context than just rugby football.

Yet when South Africa was readmitted to international rugby in 1992 after the years of isolation, I felt the task confronting us was immense. We quickly had to learn about international rugby again. We were still quite competitive in terms of pure rugby playing despite isolation, because of our competitive Currie Cup programme. Yet we soon found out what the apartheid era had cost us in a rugby sense when we went out into the wider world and played on that stage. The truth was, we were well behind the other countries.

Therefore, we had to catch up and learn and we did that rather quickly. But then, we had to; we were staging the World Cup just three years later. So much expectation existed within our country regarding that tournament.

In the absence of international rugby, the game in the provincial arena within South Africa had become almost tribal with provinces playing each other in front of 50,000 crowds. But then, once we were readmitted, South African rugby had new horizons to pursue, starting with the southern hemisphere's Super 10 tournament in 1993. Transvaal, the team I captained, did very well and beat Auckland 20-17 in the final. Some key players, such as Pieter Hendriks, Japie Mulder, Hennie Le Roux, Balie Swart, Kobus Wiese and myself would go on to play in the World Cup final two years later.

The following year, 1994, Natal reached the final of the Super 10 tournament before going down 21-10 to Queensland in Durban. It meant a lot of our

Opposite: François Pienaar the talismanic captain who led the Springbok team back onto world stage.

189

François Pienaar

leading players were gaining much needed experience from that. We needed to play international rugby, to go overseas again and encounter the difficulties of that process. It also gave us an insight into the standards that existed in New Zealand and Australia, both of which countries were sure to be leading contenders for the 1995 World Cup.

In 1994, I went on my first major tour to that part of the world for a three-match Test series against New Zealand. It was a very tough tour with a lot of controversies and we lost it, 2-0 with the third Test drawn 18-all. But for me, the most valuable factor was the incredibly steep learning curve we were still engaged upon. It gave me much food for thought and the draw in the final Test, a match we were unlucky not to win, provided a nice platform on which to build.

By the time 1995 arrived, I knew we would be a young team going into what was an extremely important tournament for the whole of South Africa. I did not minimize the value of the event in any sense. It is not necessary to go through all the fine details of that World Cup here: everybody knows what happened. But suffice to say, South Africa were not the favourites going into that World Cup, Australia were. In my mind, they were an unbelievable team. Therefore, to upset them in the first game was very important. After that, there was always the belief in my mind that we could go all the way and so it turned out. But of course, finals are always tough and they can come down to just one missed tackle or one successful kick.

It was an incredibly emotional experience at the final whistle in that 1995 final, although I never rejoiced openly after a win. It was only really later that I got the whole picture as to what it actually meant to the entire country.

And even today, twelve years later, when I drive around South Africa, people still recognize me and still talk about that day and what it meant for the country. It was a special moment and we had our place in the sun.

And what of our legacy? It is not for me to say whether the legacy has matched that achievement. But I would have to say, look at the curve in the last ten years and it has not been a great trend compared to the other countries. That is disappointing for we have the talent definitely to be in the top three in the world, if not the top two.

One reason for that is, the outstanding team that had won the World Cup, was dismantled prematurely. South Africa was just starting to play the type of rugby that could have led the world game. We had a massive performance against England at Twickenham at the end of 1995, beating them 24-14. But breaking it up too soon meant that side never really peaked.

Something else I should say is that professionals had destroyed South African rugby for a long period. That spell of professionalism was badly managed and I include the players in that criticism. To my mind, no-one in South African rugby has yet grasped the concept of professional rugby and what it really means. It is not about money, it is about being professional in the way you behave, what you do, how seriously you take your work, how you prepare yourself for training, matches or the organization of the game.

As for the future for the game in South Africa, I believe we can anticipate a great era. We have seen in the last couple of years stars coming through and their achievements have grabbed the imagination of the world. I just hope for the sake of rugby in South Africa that those star players will be able to realize their full potential.

For the fact is, I still love this game and always will do. And my feelings are shared by countless numbers of people in the new South Africa.

'It was an incredibly emotional experience at the final whistle in that 1995 final'. The usually reticent Pienaar raises his arms in triumph as South Africa win the Webb Ellis trophy on their first attempt and on home soil.

2000s:
The Game Since Professionalism

2000s: The Game Since Professionalism

Given that New Zealand's population tops just three million, you have to admire the way the country has consistently utilized the human pool of talent at its disposal. The hunger, drive and determination of New Zealand's rugby players, not to mention their excellence and technical proficiency, know no limits.

There are few teams that might have pretensions to the title of being the greatest rugby nation of the last sixty years, and especially since professionalism arrived. True, they have not won a World Cup from 1987 to 2011, yet in every other respect they stand supreme at the head of the game.

Their last four tours to the northern hemisphere have all ended in Grand Slams. Indeed, under the shrewd coaching eye of Graham Henry, New Zealand have won forty-four of their last forty-six matches against northern hemisphere opposition, a statistic of startling supremacy and indeed clarity. Such a record brooks no arguments.

In the southern hemisphere's Tri-Nations competition, they have won in seven of the last nine years. No one in world rugby can boast a period of such sustained excellence.

The All Blacks' coaching triumvirate of Graham Henry, Steve Hansen and Wayne Smith took New Zealand into the 2011 World Cup with high hopes of at last winning the William Webb Ellis trophy for the first time in twenty-four years.

But should you judge a nation solely on World Cups? Is it a fair and reasonable assessment to look only at a single competition? Or should other tournaments, plus factors such as the ability to sustain success and quality over a long period of time, be more accurate and worthy arbiters?

For me, a side can get lucky and win a World Cup. Or it might simply be enjoying a one-off golden era, blessed by a cluster of world-class players all emerging at the same time. That happens. But I believe the greatest test of any sporting team or individual is an ability to back up triumphs, again and again.

Plenty of countries have enjoyed their place in the sun since professionalism arrived in rugby in 1995. But few have stayed there.

South Africa, perhaps, lays the next best claim after New Zealand, for they won World Cups in 1995 and 2007. But in other competitions, their form fluctuated wildly: Tri-Nations champions in 2004, then bottom of that competition in 2006, 2007 and 2008. They were champions again in 2009, but bottom once more in 2010. This, surely, is not the record of a side to be revered. Respected, yes, in terms of some outstanding individual players, but collectively as a team they have too often been erratic and underperformed.

In 1999, Australia became the first country to lift the coveted William Webb Ellis trophy twice, following their 1991 World Cup triumph. Given their comparatively small playing base, Australia has done tremendously well over the course of the last

They won successive Tri-Nations titles in 2005, 2006, 2007 and 2008 before South Africa broke the run in 2009. But twelve months later, after a difficult year, the New Zealanders revived, again lifting the trophy, their fifth in six years.

The New Zealanders embarked upon a series of tours of the northern hemisphere that brought them unbroken successes in the first decade of the 21st century. Not only did Grand Slams against the home unions become commonplace but ritual slayings of the French also became the norm, not the exception.

In 2006, the French were wiped off the field in Lyon in a Test match so one-sided it brought shame and humiliation to the locals. New Zealand won 47-3 with what it seemed at the time was almost a freak show, a one-off performance of exquisite excellence.

Yet just three years later, the New Zealanders were at it again, demolishing France 39-12 at Marseille's Vélodrome stadium. It was yet another singular performance of outstanding technique, precision of execution and control. On both occasions, the French seemed unable to know what to do about it.

There was none of the traditional French forward fire and spirit. Behind the scrum, France appeared also to have lost the intuitive brilliance of their three-quarters. Those off-the-cuff skills had lit up world rugby through the years, but suddenly French rugby seemed somehow formulaic and predictable. For sure, it was cleaner and the villains had been expunged from the scene. But so much of the French character had gone with them.

Humiliations came thick and fast for the other northern hemisphere countries, too, from 2005 to 2010. Ireland were annihilated 66-28 by New Zealand in New Plymouth in June 2010, albeit after No. 8 Jamie Heaslip had been sent off. But the other home countries faced similar embarrassments when the New Zealanders turned up.

Scotland, who lost 32-6 to them in Edinburgh in 2008, went down 49-3 at Murrayfield in November 2010. In seven matches against the All Blacks from 2005 to 2010, England lost every one and conceded a total of 222 points in those seven games.

For Wales, it was a similar story. They also met the All Blacks seven times from 2005 to 2010 and conceded 242 points in those games, also losing every one. The New Zealand chariot seemed unstoppable.

Frank Bunce, an All Black of great quality who won 55 caps as a centre from 1990 to 97, reflected on what it means to be an All Black: 'Well, for a start, the long held appetite in our country to become an All Black is as strong as ever. That has never diminished. Professional rugby players sometimes get criticized after a bad performance for only being in the game for the money, but the truth is, in New Zealand, the fire and desire to be an All Black still burn as fiercely as they ever did. You want to do the best for that jersey. Another factor is, I think we have an inherent advantage. We have a lot of natural skill and ball talent in our country. Perhaps it's the influence of the Maoris and Pacific island families, but other countries don't have that. A lot of these people can do things with a ball without any training. Plus, we are an outdoors nation. All these things give us a little bit of an edge.'

The Tri-Nations

Only twice since 2004, when South Africa won the tournament in Jake White's first year as Springbok coach and his replacement, Peter de Villiers, guided them to the 2009 title, has either South Africa or Australia won what is the world's premier international tournament outside the World Cup. As All Blacks coach Graham Henry said in 2008, 'Our Tri-Nations games against Australia and New Zealand are much the toughest Tests we play anywhere in the world. I greatly respect the history and tradition of the Six Nations but the rugby isn't anywhere near as tough.'

In 2004, South Africa won the competition thanks chiefly to a hat-trick of tries by centre Marius Joubert in the key game against the All Blacks in Johannesburg, which inspired South Africa to a 40-26 win that set up their triumph. It was another engrossing instalment in their long-standing tussle. These great old rivals hammer six bells out of each other whenever they meet, grimacing and snarling with intent, on the rugby fields of the world. In 2005 in a match of frightening physical brutality at Cape Town, South Africa won 22-16 after Springbok lock Victor Matfield had hit All Blacks scrum-half Byron Kelleher so hard in one tackle he knocked him out cold.

The Springboks thought they'd repeated the trick when the sides met for the return in freezing Dunedin. But New Zealand snatched the game at the death, 31-27, thanks to a try by hooker Keven Mealamu. The following year, New Zealand seemed to be dominating the contest with wins in Wellington and Pretoria. But in little Rustenburg, north-west of Johannesburg and not far from the border with Botswana, South Africa squeezed out a 21-20 win that, albeit briefly, turned the tables.

Another of the world's great back-row players, Australian captain Rocky Elsom, scores at the posts against South Africa in the 2010 Tri-Nations tournament in Bloemfontein.

those of other players in the squad took England to the summit of the world game. Excellent performances were plentiful in the first three years of the 2000s. England were Six Nations Champions in 2000 and 2001, and achieved extraordinary results along the way. In 2000, Ireland were humiliated 50-18 at Twickenham, Wales humbled 46-12. England won in Paris and Rome, too, but missed out on the Grand Slam by slipping and sliding their way to a 19-13 upset in poor conditions against the marvellously feisty Scots at Murrayfield.

If there was one match that epitomized England's steely resolve to achieve, their ability in this era to take on the best and beat them whatever the circumstances or surroundings, it had to be the match against New Zealand at Wellington in 2003. There can never be excuses when you play New Zealand: for every nation, it is Judgement Day. You either stand tall and perform or succumb to defeat.

At one point in that game, England were reduced to thirteen men after two players had been sent to the sin bin. But they held firm against the fury and might of a full New Zealand side, resisting the will of the All Blacks in their own backyard with as commendable a display of character, guts and sheer will as you could ever see. England eventually won 15-13, a victory that confirmed their position as the best team in the world at that time. One week later, they earned a comprehensive 25-14 win over Australia in Melbourne, to emphasize the point.

> 'We have done more than enough to win this World Cup, it should be over. Now let's go and finish the job.'

Then there was England's 53-3 annihilation of South Africa at Twickenham in 2002, a match of such physical brutality and mental anguish for the South Africans that their captain, Corné Krige, was in tears from the pain and humiliation in the dressing room afterwards. But the greatest irony was that by the time they went to Australia for the 2003 Rugby World Cup, they had clearly peaked and were past their best.

Nonetheless, they carried that ascendancy into the tournament. Ultimately, it proved enough, but only because England had such an inspirational leader in Johnson. Late in normal time, after English fumblings and hesitancy had squandered the opportunity to despatch an inferior Australian side much earlier, Johnson stood tall. In the moments before extra time began, the scores locked at 14-14 after eighty minutes, Johnson calmly told his team, 'We have done more than enough to win this World Cup, it should be over. Now let's go and finish the job.'

They did, but only after the England captain had steadied his team's growing nerves, taking responsibility and winning crucial line-outs at vital moments. Wilkinson's drop goal finally nailed the Wallabies and England were into the record books for ever.

It was both vindication of the RFU's unprecedented backing for Woodward and confirmation that the best had been seen of this great England side. The

truth was it had been at its best more than a year before yet had still been good enough to hang on through to the World Cup the following October and win it. Only special teams can achieve such feats.

In the wake of their triumph England's demise was inevitable. They lost key men like Johnson, Wilkinson, Hill and Back and the blow was compounded by a lack of ruthlessness in recognizing the need to rebuild in time for 2007. Other countries took up the challenge.

The organization of the 2003 World Cup in Australia had been superb. France had much to do to match it in 2007, but they managed it with aplomb and were wonderful hosts. However, the 2007 Rugby World Cup will not be remembered as a classic on account of the quality of the rugby.

South Africa won it by playing an ultra-conservative game, based on a massive pack and a kicking outside-half, Butch James. They took few risks and in the final against England star wing Bryan Habana, the most exciting back-line runner in the world, received just one pass.

The Springboks had thrashed England, the defending champions, 36-0 in

Jonny Wilkinson reels away in celebration as his drop kick ensures England win the William Webb Ellis trophy in 2003, the first northern hemisphere team to do so.

an early pool match yet astonishingly, from those depths, England dragged themselves back up to the heady heights of a place in the final. Along the way, they ground out victories by means of their heavy pack of forwards over the Australians in the quarter-final at Marseille and then the French in the semi-final in Paris. But it was hardly thrilling.

Meanwhile, South Africa had a fright when the exciting, unpredictable Fijians got to 20-20 in the quarter-final in Marseille. But Fiji then missed a clear chance of a try that could have broken the Springboks and South Africa rode out the storm to win 37-20. In the semi-final against Argentina, the other big success story of the event, Jake White's side always had just too much power and quality for the South Americans.

New Zealand had been the highest-profile victims, losing to France in a quarter-final at Cardiff, after Yannick Jauzion had scored a crucial try following a clear forward pass. It meant another World Cup failure for the All Blacks.

The final, between England and South Africa, was a kicking fest, Percy Montgomery's boot triumphing over Jonny Wilkinson's for England in a 15-6 win. But those who said nothing needed to change in rugby were deluding themselves on this evidence.

There was not a lot of running rugby by Argentina in the 2007 World Cup. Prodigious kicking was the basis of their outstanding tournament, but here back-row forward Juan Manuel Leguizamón evades the challenges of French full-back Clément Poitrenaud (left) and flanker Yannick Nyanga (right) in the third-place match in Paris. Argentina won 34-10.

The tournament also confirmed the struggle of the smaller nations to keep up with the top countries in the professional era. Ireland and Wales were notable failures.

The few bright lights were supplied mainly by Fiji, who played some superb attacking rugby. Argentina did wonderfully, finishing third, but they too played a largely conservative game, relying heavily on the kicking of their fly-half Juan Martín Hernández and the goal kicking of Felipe Contepomi.

The rugby world will watch in 2011 to see whether the likes of Argentina, Samoa, Fiji, Japan and Georgia can again produce some real contests for the traditionally more powerful nations.

The Six Nations Championship

In 2000, France played a home series against New Zealand. The French lost the first Test in Paris 39-26 but squared the series with a powerful performance in the second Test at Marseille, winning 42-33. It was a reminder to the All Blacks that the French were dangerous, just as they had been when they came so gloriously from behind to topple the All Blacks in the second half of the 1999 Rugby World Cup semi-final at Twickenham.

The French have always been regarded as dangerous and enjoyed some significant successes in the 2000s. They won the Grand Slam in 2002 and 2004 and were Six Nations Champions in 2006 and 2007. They overwhelmed most opponents, beating Scotland in nine of their last ten games successively, including a 38-3 hammering in Paris in 2003. No surprise, then, that when the two countries met in the World Cup later that year, France won 51-9 and followed it up with a 31-0 hiding at Murrayfield in the Six Nations of 2004 and a 46-19 win three years later.

England inflicted similar humiliations on the hapless Scots, scoring 43, 29, 40, 35 and 43 points against them from 2001 to 2005. Encouragingly for the Scots, however, the arrival of Frank Hadden as coach in time for the 2006 Six Nations brought better results. Both France and England were beaten at Murrayfield in 2006, much needed wins for a nation that is struggling badly to stay in touch with the leading rugby countries of the world due to a reduced player base.

The other Celtic nations have enjoyed more success. A long-awaited Grand Slam for Wales in 2005, their first for twenty-seven years, was greeted with raucous acclaim, and followed by another in 2008. Welsh rugby had known some tough times in that intervening period, but to see the enthusiasm, passion and interest come once more to life in a manner that perhaps only the Welsh can demonstrate was a marvellous experience.

Since then, however, Welsh rugby has again stumbled. In the 2009 Six Nations, they started brightly with wins over Scotland and England. But defeat to France in Paris set them back, followed by a home defeat at the hands of Ireland.

The 2010 Championship was one step worse for Warren Gatland's men. They lost to England, France and Ireland and this decline was underlined in late 2010 when they failed to win any of their four autumn internationals against sides from the southern hemisphere. A 16-16 draw with Fiji was their best effort in a poor year. Wales were starting to underachieve big time.

As for Ireland, they went into 2007, World Cup year, as the most obviously talented and consistent side in Europe. Triple Crowns in 2004, 2006 and 2007, as well as four successive victories over England in 2004, 2005, 2006 and 2007, plus defeats of South Africa and Australia in November 2006, emphasized their progress.

The Irish have had world-class talent in players like Brian O'Driscoll and Paul O'Connell. Now, though, they have found more players of proper international ability to enhance their overall strength. In summer 2008, they replaced Eddie O'Sullivan as coach with Munster's Declan Kidney. Ireland's bitterly disappointing failure at the 2007 World Cup sealed O'Sullivan's fate. In 2009, Irish rugby reached its modern pinnacle. No Irish team had won a Grand Slam since Karl Mullen's side way back in 1948 but now, under Brian O'Driscoll's continuing encouragement, excellence and captaincy, they finally did it.

The campaign started with a 30-21 win over France in Dublin and continued with a routine 38-9 win in Italy. They were clear favourites to beat England in Dublin, but in the event it proved a terrific battle. Typically, it was O'Driscoll who again roused his men with a try, but Delon Armitage's try for England ensured a terrific finish.

Ireland held on by their fingernails for a 14-13 win and relief flooded Croke Park. They then negotiated a tricky hurdle in Scotland, winning 22-15 before the Grand Slam decider against Wales in Cardiff on the final day of the season.

It was a tight, nervous affair but at 17-15, with only seconds remaining, Ireland seemed safe. Yet then came great drama. English referee Wayne Barnes awarded Wales a last-minute penalty and up stepped Stephen Jones, who had already kicked four penalties and dropped a goal.

Yet the kick was from around 50 metres, at the extremity of Jones's range. A surer bet seemed to be long-range kicker Gavin Henson, yet Jones took the kick. His effort was just short and Ireland had done it, to the unconfined joy of an entire nation.

The Six Nations has continued to attract sell-out crowds, huge TV money and great income. But as Will Greenwood, England's centre at the 2003 Rugby World Cup, wrote after the 2007 tournament, 'Both France and Ireland's inability to claim the Grand Slam – the third successive season without a clean sweep – said it all. Here was a tournament with some excellent rugby, superb individual performances and dramatic climaxes, yet no one side was capable of stamping their absolute authority or proceedings and lifting themselves above the pack. It was a Championship that failed, albeit narrowly, to fire on all cylinders.'

This was becoming a pattern, a disturbing trend. Not since the early years of the 2000s, when England played brilliant attacking rugby at searing pace, had there been such impressive rugby. But Wales deserved huge credit for landing Grand Slams in 2005 and 2008. They were far from the finished product, yet

The French team celebrates winning the 2010 Six Nations after defeating England in the tournament's final match.

their sense of inspiration, pride and adventure was enough to take them to the top of European rugby twice in four seasons. Shane Williams, their exciting wing three-quarter, played a huge role in those Grand Slam triumphs and was voted International Rugby Board Player of the Year in 2008.

England, by contrast, despite their huge playing and financial resources, had not won a Grand Slam since 2003, nor France since 2004. Europe's big two had clearly lost their way. In 2003, England had some crushing wins, beating Scotland 40-9, Wales 26-9, France 25-17 and finishing off with a 42-6 thrashing of Ireland in Dublin. But the Irish have long memories. They beat England for the next four years in the Six Nations Championship, culminating in a 43-13 hiding, their biggest ever, on a memorable night at Croke Park in 2007. Only in 2008 did England win again.

However, France finally came good in the 2010 tournament, winning their first Grand Slam since 2004. Yet they had a shocking case of stage fright on the big night, retreating completely into their shells in the deciding match against England in Paris, the last match of the tournament that year.

France had been too strong for everyone else, beating Scotland 18-9 in Edinburgh, Ireland 33-10 in Paris, Wales 26-20 in Cardiff and Italy 46-20 in Paris. But a strange thing happened against England on a night of raw emotions at the Stade de France on 20 March. England, hitherto poor and unconvincing, suddenly revealed another side to their game, opening up and attacking the French, who immediately panicked.

Chris Ashton dives over for one of his record-breaking four tries in England's 2011 Six Nations 59-13 win over Italy. England went on to win the Championship for the first time in eight years. But their heavy 24-8 defeat by Ireland dashed their Grand Slam hopes.

Exciting full-back Ben Foden scored a fine try for England and only some English indiscipline, which gave French scrum-half Morgan Parra three penalty goals, kept the French in front.

But their game had atrophied, whereas England's, until that time largely sterile and ponderous, suddenly flourished. England began to pour out of defence with ball in hand and the sight terrified the panicking French. It was only the fact that England were not used to this style of rugby that prevented them finishing off at least two or more clear try-scoring opportunities.

Those missed chances proved crucial. The French, playing like an England team of old by focusing only on the forwards with a pair of kicking half-backs, somehow hung on for a narrow 12-10 win.

But the match had shown that it was perhaps England who were better suited to adapting to the new law interpretations than the French.

England won the 2011 Six Nations Championship for the first time in eight years. But their heavy 24-8 defeat on the final day of the season in Ireland dashed their Grand Slam hopes and revealed that they still had far to go as a developing team. Overall, it was an ordinary Six Nations, with none of the countries showing sustained excellence. Certainly in a technical sense, it seemed there was little to frighten the leading nations of the southern hemisphere.

The Future

There have been some compelling matches in the northern hemisphere down the years from 2000, but too many were increasingly dominated by kicking, especially penalties. In effect, referees were deciding matches, as in October 2008, when an adventurous Bath side went to Toulouse and led the French champions 16-15 going into injury time in an exciting Heineken Cup tie. But, as was becoming increasingly frequent, a late decision by the referee settled the match. Ireland's George Clancy awarded Toulouse a penalty and, with the final kick of the game, David Skrela landed it to squeeze Toulouse home 18-16. This was a familiar pattern throughout the northern hemisphere, penalties winning games. It was why the IRB wanted to look at some new laws to try and change such an unsatisfactory state of affairs.

The new law interpretations have been a profound encouragement to those sides willing to embrace a more ball-in-hand running style of rugby than the kicking fest that dominated the game previously. The new philosophy gave the advantage to the ball carrier rather than the tackler or defender at the breakdown.

Players who had constantly been guilty of sealing off the ball at the ruck, or at least delaying its release to slow down the game, found themselves targeted by referees. And given the intimidating fitness levels of the modern professional teams, to lose a player to the sin bin for ten minutes had a huge effect.

This was a very welcome step forward for the game and another came with the close attention paid to advancing players at the kick ahead. Aimless kicking downfield had begun to blight the game because opponents receiving the kick invariably found themselves confronted by a wall of defenders. Hence, most would lamely return the kick rather than risk running it back and conceding a turnover in contact.

But suddenly referees began to enforce a law that said every kicker of the ball must lead the chase for it. Anyone moving ahead of him is offside. This meant that a downfield kick began to be a liability because defenders receiving the ball were afforded metres more space in which to counter attack.

The best teams, like New Zealand, took full advantage of these new law interpretations. And, as ever, they led the way in showing the sport there was potentially a whole new, better game out there just waiting to be played.

Martin Johnson
England 1993–2003
Lock Forward

Martin Johnson led England to their greatest triumph, the 2003 Rugby World Cup, which climaxed a magnificent career. He won 84 caps for England, making his debut against France in 1993. At 2.01 metres and 119 kg, Johnson was a powerful lock forward and an inspiration with his quiet, firm leadership for Leicester and England.

'I played with so many fine players and was lucky enough to enjoy much success. I can hardly begin to say how fortunate I was.

Was England's World Cup-winning side its best team? After all, in 2001 we scored most tries in the Championship but we didn't win it.

To me, peaking is when you win the game. In 2003 we lost only one game, when we sent out ten reserves against France in Marseille. That was the best season.

Maybe we played the more entertaining rugby in the two years before that. But you cannot ignore results. In 2003, we won the Grand Slam and then beat New Zealand and Australia on a southern hemisphere tour, on consecutive weekends. That is the only time England has managed that. We couldn't have been in a much better position going into that World Cup.

We were a team better at winning those close games than we were the one-sided ones. When we lost to Ireland in 2001 in Dublin, we just tried to play too much rugby. Always remember, you have to win the game first. That still applies as much as ever; you must win first.

New Zealand today plays a high-pressure game and puts teams under a lot of pressure. That is what rugby is all about. We just did whatever we could to win the game. It is the sign of a good team whatever the conditions, whatever needs to be done you try and do it.

That summer tour to New Zealand and Australia in 2003 underlined that. We won the game in Wellington in conditions of pouring rain and mud, then the following week we played indoors against Australia in Melbourne and won again. We played a completely different way in the second game but still won. That is the sign of a good team when you can win in all circumstances and conditions.

Opposite: 'There was never any doubt in my mind that we would win that final. Not even when we were held at the end of normal time.' Martin Johnson reflecting on England's 2003 World Cup triumph.

Martin Johnson

Martin Johnson

What won the World Cup? The experience of the players? There was a lot more to it than that. A lot of effort and preparation by the coaches went into it and a lot of hard work by the players. People from outside try to see who or what was the decisive influence but it is difficult to be exact and put your finger on exactly who did what and how important that was to the overall achievement. But I would say Clive Woodward was always very much someone who could see the big picture and that was a major factor. He was clever and innovative. And he was desperately keen to be successful and win.

We had a lot of good players, of course, in terms of skills, but they were hard workers too; their work ethic was second to none. We didn't have guys that got carried away when they won a match or two.

And with hindsight maybe the fact that we had lost some crucial games along the way to the World Cup kept us hungry and focused. Maybe we wouldn't have been so determined had we won two or three Grand Slams on the trot in the Championship. Perhaps those results, like losing to Scotland in 2000, to Ireland in 2001 and to France in 2002, helped us keep a perspective.

When I look back, the satisfaction at our World Cup win comes from the fact that we matched the expectation put on us. We were the best team in the world and we justified that billing by ending up winners. We dealt with a lot too: going away from home, dealing with the grief, the anti-Englishness you get, the fuss made over having sixteen players on the field against Samoa... things like that.

We had to try and handle all that stupid stuff and put it out of our minds. We overcame all that and kept concentrating on winning games. That factor gives me a lot of satisfaction.

There was never any doubt in my mind that we would win that final. Not even when we were held at the end of normal time. When we got into the huddle before extra time began, I looked in our guys' eyes and saw their body language. I saw their reaction to the thought of another test before us and I knew we were going to win. It's easy to say that now, but I honestly believed it at the time, too. I vividly remember looking at them and thinking to myself we are going to win this game.

Australia was a good team, but I felt that whatever they could have done, we would have matched them. Of course, we should have had the game won before then, we should have put it away in normal time. But we made mistakes; there were some refereeing decisions that were strange and other factors combined to prevent that. But you have to find a way past those difficulties and we did that.

The RFU also deserved credit for the part they played. They stuck with Clive Woodward after 1999, when so much of the media was demanding he be sacked.

For me it was always about just playing rugby. And the experiences we had when we were out in Australia kept things in perspective for us. The most pressurized game of that entire tournament for us was against South Africa in the pool match in Perth. The pressure was really on for that one, yet it was played against a backdrop of the wife of one of our players, Will Greenwood, being in danger of losing their child back in England. So you have to keep things in perspective: we were just playing a few games of rugby. How did they compare in importance to what Will and his wife were going through?

Rugby today is still a great sport with a huge amount of integrity. There are certain non-negotiable aspects contained within its charter. People said to me after the World Cup final, how did you keep your players from reacting against the referee? But this is rugby, you don't do those things. You don't argue with referees. There is a great integrity about the game and you strive to keep that.

When I look back on my career, I don't necessarily think about just the obvious highlights, because your low points were also part of it all. That's life: you can't enjoy the high points if you haven't known low points as well. That is all part of your career, your life.

Martin Johnson can't contain his elation at the final whistle of the 2003 World Cup final.

Dan Carter

New Zealand 2003–present
Full-back

Dan Carter made his All Blacks debut in 2003. Since then, he has developed into an outstanding goal kicker and points scorer, one of the best in the history of the game. He is also a supreme player: quick, neat, calm and skilful, with superb game management.

I never dared to dream that one day I would play in a World Cup. That would have been raising your hopes far too high as a youngster.

I remember, too, New Zealand wing John Kirwan's famous try in the pool match against Italy in that tournament, when he seemed to beat most of the Italian side as he ran almost the length of the field. I was at home in Southbridge, where I grew up, 28 miles south-west of Christchurch, and as soon as JK scored that try, we youngsters who had seen it on TV got into the backyard and tried to do the same. My mates and I had great fun trying to do something similar.

I think it sums up the enjoyment rugby always gave me, from when I was young and first started playing. You were outside the house, in the backyard, playing with your friends, and whether there were two of you or up to fifteen or twenty, we were always throwing a ball around. That was why I loved it.

But another reason was I love the team ethic of rugby. It isn't and it can't be just down to individuals. Take John Kirwan's try. Good as it was, someone else had to win the ball for him to start running with it. That is the essence of rugby, what makes it so special. It is a real team game, with everyone playing their part.

For me it is the team thing that is the best. Playing alongside your mates, working towards the same goals and the friendships you create are all integral parts of this game. You play with or against a lot of fellow players, coaches, managers and other people associated with the game, and you generate a lot of friendships from among all those people. To me, that is fantastic; that is the beauty of a team sport.

Of course, you also get to travel a lot and that means you make friends all over your own country, but also around the world. I just think rugby is very special from that point of view. Yet it is a curious phenomenon. For rugby as a sport is a really brutal, physical game, yet once the final whistle goes, all that brutality is left behind on the field and you can enjoy talking about the game with the people you played against. That means there is a real respect there.

Dan Carter

Opposite: Dan Carter demonstrates his raw power as it takes two French defenders to slow him.

217

Dan Carter

I suppose another way of putting that would be to ask, did the game lose something by going pro? And I think the answer is, no, I don't think so. First of all, it has opened up a lot of employment opportunities to all manner of people in a lot of areas, like managing, coaching, playing etc. There are job opportunities for people that love rugby.

And as regards the values of the game in the old amateur era and now the professional world, I know my values are very similar to those of many other people. I don't think the game has lost those values in the transition to professionalism. I'm not sure I would enjoy playing it as much as I do had it done so.

Yes, it would have been fun playing in the amateur era, but a lot of hard work too. Those guys from that time had jobs and also had rugby. Then there was the travel. It must have been a huge commitment and quite tough for them. You hear a few stories from the very old days about guys going away on tours by ship and being away from home for five months or more. But they would have made great friendships on those tours, there would have been a lot of that.

To be able to play the game you love, for the country you love, and also call it your job makes you very fortunate. I am under no illusions as regards that.

Of course, it would be a lot easier without all the attention from the media, which has grown so much in recent years. But I see that as all part of the game, the way things are. But you couldn't say it is a problem, for as a player you can still get on with your job without having to worry too much about it.

For my senior All Blacks Test debut against Wales in 2003 there was a lot of excitement twenty-four hours before that game and I was very nervous. My lifelong dream was about to come true; it was a great moment.

Yet I do remember I slept pretty well, despite the nerves. But then I can always do that; I'm fortunate in that respect, because it is a great help to sleep well.

When you work extremely hard for something over a long period of time and it is about to become reality, it is pretty special. And I know I am one of the lucky few to have played rugby for New Zealand. That will always be a cherished, special feeling.

And that sense of excitement has never left me, I'm pleased to say. The game I love continues to give me a lot of enjoyment and the excitement comes from wearing the black jersey. Every time I get that All Black jersey in my hands, I feel that excitement. But it is a responsibility, too, because I know I am representing my country and contributing to the great legacy that came before me.

But playing alongside Richie McCaw for several years has left me with a deep respect for him. He is a very special rugby player. He has won everything and is respected all over the world. Not every player earns that sort of respect, by any means. He puts his body on the line every time he goes onto the field, no matter which jersey he is wearing. And it motivates you as a player when you see the hard work he puts in, both on and off the field.

Another guy I always admired was Jonah Lomu. I never got to play with him but he was such a special athlete. He was unique; there was no one like him before and I am not sure there will ever be anyone like him again. He was big, powerful and fast, which was a fearsome combination for opponents facing him. He was a rare talent, an awesome guy to confront on the field, I imagine.

Dan Carter lines up a kick against Wales in a 2010 international. Few doubt Carter won't be international rugby's highest points scorer.

The Future
of the Game

'Clubs who collectively used to put out ten or twelve teams each week have now banded together but they're struggling even to raise a single side. That's how bad it is.'

There are, says Upsdell, many reasons for this alarming state of affairs.

Osterley used to attract a lot of their players from local schools but the decline in rugby in schools has meant that that supply line has dried up. 'Schools don't play rugby around here any more and everywhere kids play less. Professionalism has just widened the divide between the top and junior clubs.'

A Middlesex official admitted that there was widespread dismay and sadness once Osterley's plight had been revealed. But, he said, 'The biggest problems began when so many schools stopped playing rugby. This had a dramatic effect on the adult population. And to make matters worse, at many clubs now you can't find the officials to give voluntary time to administer the game.

'Another big difficulty is the number of kids who give up the game from 16 to 18. The RFU has had to recognize that among all the rugby-playing nations the performance in England of governing the transformation from thousands of kids playing mini rugby to junior club rugby was the worst in the world. We are absolutely hopeless at it. When that problem was identified, the RFU focused resources on the clubs rather than the schools to keep kids playing rugby. But that was a mistake.'

A sad one-off case of an English junior club failing to adapt to the times, but of little concern to others? If only. Osterley's example is being mirrored throughout England as clubs of long-standing suffer a significant reduction in playing numbers.

Whichever way you look at it, a full house of 82,000 at Twickenham, with countless hospitality boxes stuffed full of people and millions being taken in gate receipts, is just one side of English rugby.

It is true that the English Rugby Union has spent many thousands of pounds trying to arrest this decline and, in some areas and instances, has succeeded. But the general trend is disturbing at many traditional junior clubs.

Take Northern Ireland. There, former Ireland and Lions captain Willie John McBride reports a similarly worrying pattern. 'The game is in serious decline at junior level; the picture is one of concern. Even the Irish Rugby Football Union are beginning to show concern. In 2007 and in Ulster alone there were thirty-seven less clubs playing the game.

'I know of several clubs that are struggling. One of them was my original club Randalstown. Antrim are also in difficulties and Derry, too; they're in terrible straits. They have had tough years, getting bombed out of their original home. They built a nice new clubhouse but they're struggling to keep the club afloat.'

But it isn't just the small junior clubs that have found life tough, says McBride. North of Ireland Football Club was the club of the great Jack Kyle, Noel Henderson and Mike Gibson. 'Imagine the history attached to that club,' says McBride. 'But it has gone, amalgamated with Collegians, the old pupils of Methodist College, as Belfast Harlequins. It is very sad. When I played, those teams were mighty, proud teams.'

Much the same can be said in other countries, like Wales and Scotland, where numbers playing the game are decreasing. At the end of 2006, a Magners Celtic League match was played between Glasgow Warriors and Edinburgh. It attracted a paltry, pathetic crowd of 2,613.

So how much of this is attributable to professionalism? It is too easy to point the finger solely in that direction. When you analyse it, wider problems can be detected, a point with which McBride concurs. The evolution in society in general, with its wider array of interests and hobbies, has reduced people's commitment to any single activity, and rugby has not bucked this trend. Once thriving junior cricket clubs have similarly struggled or gone to the wall.

In the modern world, easier transport links offering travel to alluring destinations, an increasingly materialistic society in which financial accumulation has attained a far greater importance, not least to meet responsibilities, and the demands of famillies have all combined to damage any sporting activity's attraction. Young people in the computer age have rival interests, too.

It is certainly true of the modern-day man in his 20s and 30s, perhaps with the responsibility of a wife and young family. To find the time in his schedule to go training two nights a week for as much as eight or nine months a year, plus play a match each weekend that may require him to be away from home for anything between eight and twelve hours, is increasingly impossible. Families are doing more together; thus, a husband keen on rugby might well go to watch a match, but perhaps take his wife with him. Then there is another element to consider: injuries.

> 'We were talking about rugby in New Zealand and the schools and he told me that there were now soccer posts at Wellington College.'

The greater focus on physicality in the game has meant many young players have rejected the sport. In New Zealand, an increasing number of mothers expressed alarm at seeing their sons compete against youngsters of a similar age from a background in the Pacific Islands, where young men grow physically bigger at a younger age. This led to many New Zealand youngsters abandoning the game, either through their parents' wishes or their own decision.

Willie John McBride remembered, 'When I toured New Zealand with the Lions in 1971, one of my adopted schools was Wellington College. I would go and talk to the kids there when we played at Wellington. A couple of years ago, I went back to New Zealand and stayed with Colin Meads, one of my great old adversaries. We were talking about rugby in New Zealand and the schools and he told me that there were now soccer posts at Wellington College. Too many parents of the white boys told their sons, "You are not playing rugby any longer, it is too dangerous." When you have that kind of situation anywhere it is damaging for the game long term.'

In France, happily, they report a 5 per cent increase in playing numbers in the last few years. There is little tradition of schools teaching the sport in the country. Youngsters wishing to take up the game join their local club at an early age and

But how might they have handled the modern game? Without adding considerable bulk, they would scarcely have lasted in ultra-physical modern rugby with its lack of time and space. And what skills and speed might they have lost had they added significant weight? Even one of the greatest flair players, the former Australian wing David Campese, conceded that the decision to enhance his physique so that he went from 82 to 92 kg in time for the 1995 World Cup greatly reduced his speed and overall effectiveness.

In the modern game, physical bulk and power have become all. Thus, the sport has evolved into something far closer to a battle of behemoths, a clash of physical giants more akin to American football or rugby league than the old amateur game where skills were of the utmost importance. This is a shame, a matter of deep regret. But perhaps these so-called battles of behemoths provide a spectacle to the tastes more suited of modern audiences. By and large, rugby union crowds of former days were altogether more knowledgeable, more appreciative of the game's finer skills, its intricacies and subtleties than modern-day audiences. But as Willie John McBride says, the composition of crowds at international matches has changed significantly. The corporate world has take over these occasions, to the growing exclusion of the true rugby supporter.

What can we expect in the future? More of the same? If that proves to be so, then the careers of the leading players will become even shorter. Serious injuries are now an everyday occurrence for those at the top of the game, and size alone is no defence against them. Players of such physical magnitude, primed to generate a pace never before within their capacity, have become explosive bundles of human danger, both to themselves and to any opponents in their way.

By the start of 2007, the game had been engaged in deep studies of these growing numbers of injuries and their implication for the sport of the future. For example, the IRB introduced a new procedure at the scrummage, aimed at eliminating the serious risk of major injury to front-row forwards at the engagement. It proposed carefully managed contact, hoping to avoid the crash of bodies hitherto seen as an integral part of the sport. The game's law-makers are right to be concerned: one paralysed young player, and there have been several around the world, is one too many.

Unfortunately, right into the year of 2011, the scrummage remained a mess. The controversial technique of 'Crouch, touch, pause, engage' showed few signs of solving a long-standing difficulty, as another World Cup year unfolded. There were still far too many scrum collapses, far too much time was being wasted trying to restart the game and the whole thing had become tiresome.

Given that at every scrum there exists the potential for serious injury such is the collision of bodies, it began to look as though scrums were becoming an unnecessary evil in the modern game.

So many serious, long-term injuries will require bigger squads and therefore greater financial outlay and commitment. Expecting any player to play much more than twenty games a season will become impossible in the future unless the physicality of the sport is reduced. And that seems unlikely.

Only with the careful management of players by the union, as has been possible in countries like New Zealand and Ireland, will players enjoy careers of longevity even approaching those of their predecessors. Without that, we are going to see players lasting only perhaps five or six years at the top level.

Already, some have voted with their feet and rejected a professional rugby career. Professionalism has forced young men of academic capabilities to choose between the game and their career. You have to say, the most sensible have gone for the career. That, too, has been to rugby's detriment.

Years of involvement in the game by future doctors, lawyers, dentists, captains of industry and financial experts brought a unique flavour to the sport. On major tours of past times, such as those of the British & Irish Lions, Welsh steelworkers and miners shared rooms with Cambridge University students or brilliant scientists. This extraordinary pot-pourri of human intellect and character defined the game. Alas, in its professional guise, there has been a levelling out and rugby union is poorer for it.

Only the naive would suggest that rugby should never have gone professional. It had to, there was no alternative. Commercial elements outside the game would have seen to that and, in their hands, no protection whatsoever would have been afforded to the old ways and customs of the sport.

But that said, it was surely disappointing that the leaders of the game abrogated so utterly their responsibilities by simply allowing a free-for-all. No business could expect salvation in its field for so crass a policy, so poorly prepared a strategy. And never forget, the moment rugby union became professional, it was first and foremost a business. This great game that has meant so much to so many the world over these last 100 years and more was surely entitled to expect something better from those with its control in their hands. The old gentlemen of the IRB merit most of the condemnation that has been directed their way since their panic decision.

But that is not to say a better future cannot be imagined. Clearly, it can. Rugby union remains a hugely popular game throughout the world, as evidenced by the rise of its flagship event, the Rugby World Cup, to a position of third top sports event in the world, behind only the FIFA Football World Cup and the Olympic Games. That is some achievement for a sport that barely a dozen years ago was losing so many of its best players to rugby league. But to achieve its complete potential in the future, the sport will need greater wisdom.

It is surely not beyond the capacity of a game that has produced so many outstanding human beings down the years to find leaders of acumen and character, people able to chart a successful path for the future.

On the field, the emphasis now surely needs to turn for the first time since professionalism arrived to the intricacies of attack. At its lively, most inventive and creative best, this game still has few equals. But the defence-riddled game that has quickly emerged these last sixteen years has damaged the wonderful side of the sport. A major rethink was required and, commendably, the IRB put in place in 2007 the possibility of such developments with the introduction of proposed major law changes. They acted after a group of the world's top coaches, some officials and players presented a case for change to an IRB Conference in Auckland in 2006. Most of these changes, 'Experimental Law Variations' (ELVs), were adopted successfully in the southern hemisphere competition of Super 14 and Tri-Nations of 2008. Alas, when the traditionalists in the northern hemisphere were asked to trial them later that year, there was an explosion of indignation and criticism. Some were trialled, but not the most important, such as the short-arm penalty awarding a free-kick or scrum for a raft of offences rather than a full penalty. Yet this idea had the potential to speed up the game and make it a significantly brighter, better spectacle.

The formidable All Blacks have retained all the elements of their traditional forward power but, unlike so many countries of the modern era, they have retained a culture of enterprise, pace and decision-making behind the scrum that was a throwback to days of yore. All credit and commendation to them under the shrewd tutelage of their coach, Graham Henry, and his knowledgeable assistants, Steve Hansen and Wayne Smith.

Another member of the hugely exciting England back three, full-back Ben Foden, is stopped by Italian centre Gonzalo Garcia in the 2011 Six Nations match between England and Italy at Twickenham. England scored eight tries and won 59-13.

New Zealand did not win the 2007 Rugby World Cup. France, their old nemesis, once more upset them, this time as early as the quarter-final stage in Cardiff, although the French only squeezed home through a try that originated from a blatant forward pass. And this World Cup mirrored too closely the previous two World Cups, won by Australia in 1999 and England in 2003, in that individual skill, decision-making and enterprise were again shunned in favour of team discipline, a cautious, tight approach and an over-reliance on goal kicking.

Clearly, defence was important, but there were increasing and encouraging signs as 2010 turned into 2011 that there was a growing focus on attack, entertainment, skill and keeping the ball in hand. Under the new law interpretations, players have been forced to make decisions for themselves based on what they see in front of them, not simply follow a coach's rigid instructions on how to play, even of fifth- or sixth-phase possession.

And yet some believe things may not be as they appear. Former Australian coach John Connolly admits there has probably been too much focus on defence in the first decade of professionalism. But, as he says, 'We have an inherent challenge in rugby. There are fifteen players on each side strung out across a 70-metre-wide field. That means you have someone standing just over every 4 metres. That being the case, the balance is inevitably on the side of defence and once professionalism arrived, it was always going to mean that professional rugby teams would become much more organized. Professionalism offered the time to perfect that organization. Yet having made that point, you still see many matches where 40 or more points are scored. Most games used to be far less than that in the old days of amateurism. You even had matches ending up 6-3 or 9-8! So that tells you the game may be freer than we think it is.'

> '...the balance is inevitably on the side of defence and once professionalism arrived, it was always going to mean that professional rugby teams would become much more organized.'

Perhaps other alterations to the laws, as urged by that great French player Jean-Pierre Rives elsewhere in this book, can help transfer the focus from defence to attack.

But on another theme, unless urgent and remedial action is taken, future World Cups may well come down to meaningful contests between only a handful of nations. Professionalism has widened the gap between the traditionally strong rugby-playing nations and the so-called lesser countries.

These smaller nations, one hastens to add, are in no way inferior in their love of and enthusiasm for the game. Indeed, some suggest they are torchbearers of what was pure rugby as a game. The tide of commercialization has yet to engulf them; indeed, some would hope it never does.

Yet without it, how can they hope even to keep up with the nations where money now fuels the entire professional game, still less match them at some undefined future point in time? The 2007 World Cup saw a repeat of some of the absurd scorelines of past tournaments: the 142-0 annihilation of Namibia by Australia in 2003, New Zealand's 101-3 flogging of Italy in 1999 and their 145-17 slaughter of Japan at the 1995 World Cup. This time, New Zealand beat Portugal 108-13, Romania 85-8 and Italy 76-14, Australia beat Japan 91-3, France beat Namibia 87-10 and Wales beat Japan 72-18... These mismatches reveal only one thing: rugby union is not in truth a sport of worldwide strength. The IRB now boasts 118 member unions with the inclusion of Iran at the end of 2010. But only a tiny percentage of the players from all these unions are serious players on the world stage. This imbalance needs to be addressed if the sport is genuinely to go forward.

Commendably, the IRB is investing some significant sums of money into most of the financially impoverished countries in a bid to raise playing levels. But greater innovation might well be required to have a profound effect. For example, why shouldn't a certain number of former internationals from countries like France and England move if they wish to, somewhere like Italy and, after a year or eighteen months' residential qualification, become available for that country? It would raise not only the playing standard, but also the entire profile of the game.

In a sport like professional soccer, where no team of a world power can be sure of reaching the last four of a World Cup, it is a different story. Playing numbers the world over ensure football's long-held position of ascendancy will remain.

Rugby is different, an altogether smaller game that badly needs strengthening around the globe in so many countries. Relaxing the rules of qualification may be one answer to what seems a long-term problem.

The danger is that the gap that currently exists will become a chasm. Today, in 2011, countries once regarded as leading rugby-playing nations like Scotland are struggling to match the pace of progression being set by the likes of New Zealand. In truth, only a tiny handful of countries have the capacity to win a World Cup. In New Zealand at the 2011 tournament, the usual suspects will dominate: New Zealand, South Africa and Australia, plus perhaps England.

It will be the game's ruling body, the IRB, that the sport will look to increasingly for leadership, guidance, wisdom and vision. Can it provide such qualities while at the same time holding the sport together for universal benefit? It will not be an easy task.

It is always better to consider the glass half full than half empty. Perhaps then, it is worth reiterating the viewpoint that this game has produced so many people of outstanding qualities that in its hour of need it will find such minds to take it forward to greater prosperity, not only for the already rich and powerful, but also for all nations that embrace the sport.

Rugby's history is littered with great deeds, acts of bravery, courage and glory by men of supreme talent, character and no small intellect. There seems no reason why it should not enjoy similarly propitious times in the future. But calm, cool heads filled with wisdom will be required to guide it towards those sunny climes, not just at the professional levels of the sport but lower down, too, if so much of what rugby always meant is to be retained for the benefit of future generations.

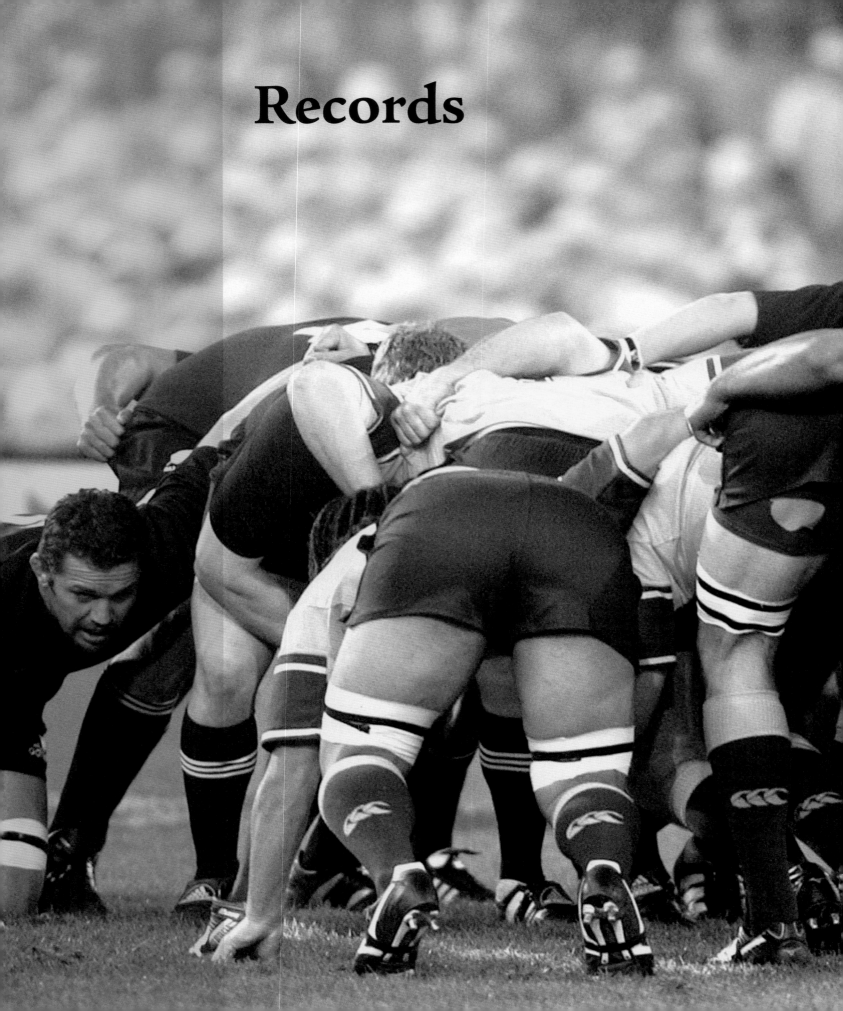

Records

British & Irish Lions Tours

1950: Australia and New Zealand
(First Post-War British Lions Tour)

Lions	9–9	New Zealand	Dunedin
Lions	0–8	New Zealand	Christchurch
Lions	3–6	New Zealand	Wellington
Lions	8–11	New Zealand	Auckland
Lions	19–6	Australia	Brisbane
Lions	24–3	Australia	Sydney

1955: South Africa

Lions	23–22	South Africa	Johannesburg
Lions	9–25	South Africa	Cape Town
Lions	9–6	South Africa	Pretoria
Lions	8–22	South Africa	Port Elizabeth

1959: Australia and New Zealand

Lions	17–6	Australia	Brisbane
Lions	24–3	Australia	Sydney
Lions	17–18	New Zealand	Dunedin
Lions	8–11	New Zealand	Wellington
Lions	8–22	New Zealand	Christchurch
Lions	9–6	New Zealand	Auckland

1962: South Africa

Lions	3–3	South Africa	Johannesburg
Lions	0–3	South Africa	Durban
Lions	3–8	South Africa	Cape Town
Lions	14–34	South Africa	Bloemfontein

1966: Australia, New Zealand and Canada

Lions	11–8	Australia	Sydney
Lions	31–0	Australia	Brisbane
Lions	3–20	New Zealand	Dunedin
Lions	12–16	New Zealand	Wellington
Lions	6–19	New Zealand	Christchurch
Lions	11–24	New Zealand	Auckland
Lions	19–8	Canada	Toronto

1968: South Africa

Lions	20–25	South Africa	Pretoria
Lions	6–6	South Africa	Port Elizabeth
Lions	6–11	South Africa	Cape Town
Lions	6–19	South Africa	Johannesburg

1971: New Zealand

Lions	9–3	New Zealand	Dunedin
Lions	12–22	New Zealand	Christchurch
Lions	13–3	New Zealand	Wellington
Lions	14–14	New Zealand	Auckland

1974: South Africa

Lions	12–3	South Africa	Cape Town
Lions	28–9	South Africa	Pretoria
Lions	26–9	South Africa	Port Elizabeth
Lions	13–13	South Africa	Johannesburg

1977: New Zealand

Lions	12–16	New Zealand	Wellington
Lions	13–9	New Zealand	Christchurch
Lions	7–19	New Zealand	Dunedin
Lions	9–10	New Zealand	Auckland

1980: South Africa

Lions	22–26	South Africa	Cape Town
Lions	19–26	South Africa	Bloemfontein
Lions	10–12	South Africa	Port Elizabeth
Lions	17–13	South Africa	Pretoria

1983: New Zealand

Lions	12–16	New Zealand	Christchurch
Lions	0–9	New Zealand	Wellington
Lions	8–15	New Zealand	Dunedin
Lions	6–38	New Zealand	Auckland

1989: Australia

Lions	12–30	Australia	Sydney
Lions	19–12	Australia	Brisbane
Lions	19–18	Australia	Sydney

1993: New Zealand

Lions	18–20	New Zealand	Christchurch
Lions	20–7	New Zealand	Wellington
Lions	13–30	New Zealand	Auckland

1997: South Africa

Lions	25–16	South Africa	Cape Town
Lions	18–15	South Africa	Durban
Lions	16–35	South Africa	Johannesburg

2001: Australia (now British & Irish Lions)

Lions	29–13	Australia	Brisbane
Lions	14–35	Australia	Melbourne
Lions	23–29	Australia	Sydney

2005: New Zealand

Lions	3–21	New Zealand	Christchurch
Lions	18–48	New Zealand	Wellington
Lions	19–38	New Zealand	Auckland

2009: South Africa

Lions	21–26	South Africa	Durban
Lions	25–28	South Africa	Pretoria
Lions	28–9	South Africa	Johannesburg

Five and Six Nations Championships

1947	Wales & England	France rejoin after WWII
1948	Ireland	Grand Slam Winners
1949	Ireland	Triple Crown Winners
1950	Wales	Grand Slam Winners
1951	Ireland	
1952	Wales	Grand Slam Winners
1953	England	
1954	England, France & Wales	England win Triple Crown
1955	France & Wales	
1956	Wales	
1957	England	Grand Slam Winners
1958	England	
1959	France	
1960	France & England	England win Triple Crown
1961	France	
1962	France	
1963	England	
1964	Scotland & Wales	
1965	Wales	Triple Crown Winners
1966	Wales	
1967	France	
1968	France	Grand Slam Winners
1969	Wales	Triple Crown Winners
1970	France & Wales	
1971	Wales	Grand Slam Winners
1972	TOURNAMENT NOT COMPLETED	
1973	Five-way tie	
1974	Ireland	
1975	Wales	
1976	Wales	Grand Slam Winners
1977	France	Grand Slam Winners, Wales win Triple Crown
1978	Wales	Grand Slam Winners
1979	Wales	Triple Crown Winners
1980	England	Grand Slam Winners

1981	France	Grand Slam Winners
1982	Ireland	Triple Crown Winners
1983	France & Ireland	
1984	Scotland	Grand Slam Winners
1985	Ireland	Triple Crown Winners
1986	France & Scotland	
1987	France	Grand Slam Winners
1988	Wales & France	Wales win Triple Crown
1989	France	
1990	Scotland	Grand Slam Winners
1991	England	Grand Slam Winners
1992	England	Grand Slam Winners
1993	France	
1994	Wales	
1995	England	Grand Slam Winners
1996	England	Triple Crown Winners
1997	France	Grand Slam Winners, England win Triple Crown
1998	France	Grand Slam Winners, England win Triple Crown
1999	Scotland	
(Competition becomes Six Nations)		
2000	England	Italy joins
2001	England	
2002	France	Grand Slam Winners, England win Triple Crown
2003	England	Grand Slam Winners
2004	France	Grand Slam Winners, Ireland win Triple Crown
2005	Wales	Grand Slam Winners
2006	France	Ireland win Triple Crown
2007	France	Ireland win Triple Crown
2008	Wales	Grand Slam Winners
2009	Ireland	Grand Slam Winners
2010	France	Grand Slam Winners
2011	England	

Rugby World Cup – William Webb Ellis Trophy

1987: NEW ZEALAND
FIRST RUGBY WORLD CUP

Quarter-finals

New Zealand	30–3	Scotland	Christchurch
France	31–16	Fiji	Auckland
Australia	33–15	Ireland	Sydney
Wales	16–3	England	Brisbane

Semi-finals

France	30–24	Australia	Sydney
New Zealand	49–6	Wales	Brisbane

Final

NEW ZEALAND	29–9	France	Auckland

1991: ENGLAND

Quarter-finals

Scotland	28–6	W. Samoa	Edinburgh
England	19–10	France	Paris
Australia	19–18	Ireland	Dublin
New Zealand	29–13	Canada	Lille

Semi-finals

England	9–6	Scotland	Edinburgh
Australia	16–6	New Zealand	Dublin

Final

AUSTRALIA	12–6	England	Twickenham

1995: SOUTH AFRICA

Quarter-finals

France	36–12	Ireland	Durban
South Africa	42–14	W. Samoa	Johannesburg
England	25–22	Australia	Cape Town
New Zealand	48–30	Scotland	Pretoria

Semi-finals

South Africa	19–15	France	Durban
New Zealand	45–29	England	Cape Town

Final

SOUTH AFRICA	15–12	New Zealand	Johannesburg

(after extra time)

1999: WALES

Quarter-finals

Australia	24–9	Wales	Cardiff
South Africa	44–21	England	Paris
New Zealand	30–18	Scotland	Edinburgh
France	47–26	Argentina	Dublin

Semi-finals

Australia	27–21	South Africa	Twickenham
France	43–31	New Zealand	Twickenham

Final

AUSTRALIA	35–12	France	Cardiff

2003: AUSTRALIA

Quarter-finals

New Zealand	29–9	South Africa	Melbourne
Australia	33–16	Scotland	Brisbane
France	43–21	Ireland	Melbourne
England	28–17	Wales	Brisbane

Semi-finals

Australia	22–10	New Zealand	Sydney
England	24–7	France	Sydney

Final

ENGLAND	20–17	Australia	Sydney

(after extra time)

2007: FRANCE

Quarter-finals

Australia	10–12	England	Marseille
New Zealand	18–20	France	Cardiff
South Africa	37–20	Fiji	Marseille
Argentina	19–13	Scotland	Paris

Semi-finals

France	9–14	England	Paris
South Africa	37–13	Argentina	Paris

Final

SOUTH AFRICA	15–6	England	Paris

Tri-Nations Series

1996	P	W	D	L	BP	Pts
New Zealand	**4**	**4**	**0**	**0**	**1**	**17**
South Africa	4	1	0	3	2	6
Australia	4	1	0	3	2	6

New Zealand	43–6	Australia	Wellington
Australia	21–16	South Africa	Sydney
New Zealand	15–11	South Africa	Christchurch
Australia	25–32	New Zealand	Brisbane
South Africa	25–19	Australia	Bloemfontein
South Africa	18–29	New Zealand	Cape Town

1997	P	W	D	L	BP	Pts
New Zealand	**4**	**4**	**0**	**0**	**2**	**18**
South Africa	4	1	0	3	3	7
Australia	4	1	0	3	2	6

South Africa	32–35	New Zealand	Johannesburg
Australia	18–33	New Zealand	Melbourne
Australia	32–20	South Africa	Brisbane
New Zealand	55–35	South Africa	Auckland
New Zealand	36–24	Australia	Dunedin
South Africa	61–22	Australia	Pretoria

1998	P	W	D	L	BP	Pts
South Africa	**4**	**4**	**0**	**0**	**1**	**17**
Australia	4	2	0	2	2	10
New Zealand	4	0	0	4	2	2

Australia	24–16	New Zealand	Melbourne
Australia	13–14	South Africa	Perth
New Zealand	3–13	South Africa	Wellington
New Zealand	23–27	Australia	Christchurch
South Africa	24–23	New Zealand	Durban
South Africa	29–15	Australia	Pretoria

1999	P	W	D	L	BP	Pts
New Zealand	**4**	**3**	**0**	**1**	**0**	**12**
Australia	4	2	0	2	2	10
South Africa	4	1	0	3	0	4

New Zealand	28–0	South Africa	Dunedin
Australia	32–6	South Africa	Brisbane
New Zealand	34–15	Australia	Auckland
South Africa	18–34	New Zealand	Pretoria
South Africa	10–9	Australia	Johannesburg
Australia	28–7	New Zealand	Sydney

2000	P	W	D	L	BP	Pts
Australia	**4**	**3**	**0**	**1**	**2**	**14**
New Zealand	4	2	0	2	4	12
South Africa	4	1	0	3	2	6

Australia	35–39	New Zealand	Sydney
New Zealand	25–12	South Africa	Christchurch
Australia	26–6	South Africa	Sydney
New Zealand	23–24	Australia	Wellington
South Africa	46–40	New Zealand	Johannesburg
South Africa	18–19	Australia	Durban

2001	P	W	D	L	BP	Pts
Australia	**4**	**2**	**1**	**1**	**1**	**11**
New Zealand	4	2	0	2	1	9
South Africa	4	1	1	2	0	6

South Africa	3–12	New Zealand	Cape Town
South Africa	20–15	Australia	Pretoria
New Zealand	15–23	Australia	Dunedin
Australia	14–14	South Africa	Perth
New Zealand	26–15	South Africa	Auckland
Australia	29–26	New Zealand	Sydney

2002	P	W	D	L	BP	Pts
New Zealand	**4**	**3**	**0**	**1**	**3**	**15**
Australia	4	2	0	2	3	11
South Africa	4	1	0	3	3	7

New Zealand	12–6	Australia	Christchurch
New Zealand	41–20	South Africa	Wellington
Australia	38–27	South Africa	Brisbane
Australia	16–14	New Zealand	Sydney
South Africa	23–30	New Zealand	Durban
South Africa	33–31	Australia	Johannesburg

2003	P	W	D	L	BP	Pts
New Zealand	**4**	**4**	**0**	**0**	**2**	**18**
Australia	4	1	0	3	2	6
South Africa	4	1	0	3	0	2

South Africa	26–22	Australia	Cape Town
South Africa	16–52	New Zealand	Pretoria
Australia	21–50	New Zealand	Sydney
Australia	29–9	South Africa	Brisbane
New Zealand	19–11	South Africa	Dunedin
New Zealand	21–17	Australia	Auckland

2004	P	W	D	L	BP	Pts
South Africa	**4**	**2**	**0**	**2**	**3**	**11**
Australia	4	2	0	2	2	10
New Zealand	4	2	0	2	1	9

New Zealand	16–7	Australia	Wellington
New Zealand	23–21	South Africa	Christchurch
Australia	30–26	South Africa	Perth

Australia	23–18	New Zealand	Sydney
South Africa	40–26	New Zealand	Johannesburg
South Africa	23–19	Australia	Durban

2005	P	W	D	L	BP	Pts
New Zealand	4	3	0	1	3	15
South Africa	4	3	0	1	1	13
Australia	4	0	0	4	3	3

South Africa	22–16	Australia	Pretoria
South Africa	22–16	New Zealand	Cape Town
Australia	13–30	New Zealand	Sydney
Australia	19–22	South Africa	Perth
New Zealand	31–27	South Africa	Dunedin
New Zealand	34–24	Australia	Auckland

2006 – Expanded tournament format introduced
(Each team played one another three times)

2006	P	W	D	L	BP	Pts
New Zealand	6	5	0	1	3	23
Australia	6	2	0	4	3	11
South Africa	6	2	0	4	1	9

South Africa	29–16	Australia	Johannesburg
South Africa	21–20	New Zealand	Rustenburg
South Africa	26–45	New Zealand	Pretoria
New Zealand	34–27	Australia	Auckland
Australia	20–18	South Africa	Sydney
Australia	9–13	New Zealand	Brisbane
New Zealand	35–17	South Africa	Wellington
Australia	49–0	South Africa	Brisbane
New Zealand	32–12	Australia	Christchurch

2007 – Reverted back to original tournament format

2007	P	W	D	L	BP	Pts
New Zealand	4	3	0	1	1	13
Australia	4	2	0	2	1	9
South Africa	4	1	0	3	1	5

South Africa	22–19	Australia	Cape Town
South Africa	21–26	New Zealand	Durban
Australia	20–15	New Zealand	Melbourne
Australia	25–17	South Africa	Sydney
New Zealand	33–6	South Africa	Christchurch
New Zealand	26–12	Australia	Auckland

2008 – Reverted back to expanded format

2008	P	W	D	L	BP	Pts
New Zealand	6	4	0	2	3	19
Australia	6	3	0	3	2	14
South Africa	6	2	0	4	2	10

| New Zealand | 19–8 | South Africa | Wellington |
| New Zealand | 28–30 | South Africa | Dunedin |

Australia	16–9	South Africa	Perth
Australia	34–19	New Zealand	Sydney
New Zealand	39–10	Australia	Auckland
South Africa	0–19	New Zealand	Cape Town
South Africa	15–27	Australia	Durban
South Africa	53–8	Australia	Johannesburg
Australia	24–28	New Zealand	Brisbane

2009	P	W	D	L	BP	Pts
South Africa	6	5	0	1	1	21
New Zealand	6	3	0	1	1	13
Australia	6	1	0	3	3	7

New Zealand	22–16	Australia	Auckland
South Africa	28–19	New Zealand	Bloemfontein
South Africa	31–19	New Zealand	Durban
South Africa	29–17	Australia	Cape Town
Australia	18–19	New Zealand	Sydney
Australia	25–32	New Zealand	Perth
Australia	21–6	South Africa	Brisbane
New Zealand	29–32	South Africa	Hamilton
New Zealand	33–6	Australia	Wellington

2010	P	W	D	L	BP	Pts
New Zealand	6	6	0	0	3	27
Australia	6	2	0	4	3	11
South Africa	6	1	0	5	3	7

New Zealand	32–12	South Africa	Auckland
New Zealand	31–17	South Africa	Wellington
Australia	30–13	South Africa	Brisbane
Australia	28–49	New Zealand	Melbourne
New Zealand	20–10	Australia	Christchurch
South Africa	22–29	New Zealand	Johannesburg
South Africa	44–31	Australia	Pretoria
South Africa	39–41	Australia	Bloemfontein
Australia	22–23	New Zealand	Sydney

ALL–TIME TRI–NATIONS TABLE

	P	W	D	L	BP	Pts
New Zealand	68	48	0	20	30	222
Australia	68	26	1	41	33	139
South Africa	68	27	1	40	23	133

POINTS SCHEDULE

Win = 4 points

Draw = 2 points

Loss = 0 points

Bonus points:

1 = scoring 4 tries in game

1 = loss by up to 7 points

Index

The publishers would like to thank the following sources for their kind permission to reproduce the pictures in this book.

Getty Images: 92–3, 105, 129, 134, 140–1, 157, 187; /AFP: 42, 76; /Shaun Botterill: 152–3, 163, 182–3, 208; /Simon Bruty: 162, 165, 167; /David Cannon: 172–3; /Central Press: 47, 51; /Central Press/Hulton Archive: 30, 52, 72-73, 80; /Russell Cheyne: 130, 177; /Jean Claude Delmas: 117; /Jacques Demarthon/AFP: 204, 229; /Franck Fife/AFP: 207; /Stu Forster: 223; /Fox Photos/Hulton Archive: 56; /Gallo Images: 199; /Georges Gobet: 143; /Bertrand Guay/AFP: 224; /Scott Heavey: 233; /Mike Hewitt: 171, 220–1; /Hulton Archive: 29b, 88, 102; /Ian Kington/AFP: 219; /Mark Kolbe: 195; /Ross Kinnaird: 178; /Nick Laham: 203; /Ross Land: 216, 242–3; /Philip Littleton/AFP: 168b; /Chris McGrath: 215; /Jean Pierre Muller/AFP: 166; /Adrian Murrell: 95, 96-97, 98–9, 136–7; /Gary M. Prior: 181; /David Rogers: 11, 159, 160, 191, 212, 227, 230, 239; /Chris Smith: 109; /Rob Taggart: 121; /Topical Press Agency/Hulton Archive: 33; /Phil Walter: 7

The New Zealand Herald: 54

Offside Sports Photography: /L'Equipe: 66, 68, 69, 79, 147, 149, 151

Press Association Images: 84–5, 101, 113; /AP: 22-23, 25, 122–3, 133; /Mike Brett: 144, 184; /Gareth Copley: 192-193; /David Davies: 4–5; /Adam Davy: 235; /Gouhier-Morton-Taamallah/ABACA: 2; /David Jones: 155; /Ross Kinnaird: 175; /Tony Marshall: 188; /S&G/Alpha: 9, 12–3, 15, 16, 18, 19, 27, 28t, 28b, 29t, 41, 44, 48–9, 58, 61, 62-63, 65, 70, 75, 83, 87b, 90, 106, 110, 114, 118, 125, 139, 256; /Kirsty Wigglesworth: 236-237

Private Collection: 34, 40, 43, 57, 60, 87t, 100, 107, 108, 112, 131, 132, 138, 142, 156, 168t, 180

Topfoto.co.uk: /Roger Viollet: 36–7

Every effort has been made to acknowledge correctly and contact the source and/or copyright holder of each picture and Carlton Books Limited apologizes for any unintentional errors or omissions, which will be corrected in future editions of this book.